Reconstructing Historical Communities

Reconstructing Historical Communities

ALAN MACFARLANE

in collaboration with Sarah Harrison and

Charles Jardine

Cambridge University Press

Cambridge

London   New York   Melbourne

Published by the Syndics of the Cambridge University Press
The Pitt Building, Trumpington Street, Cambridge CB2 1RP
Bentley House, 200 Euston Road, London NW1 2DB
32 East 57th Street, New York, NY 10022, USA
296 Beaconsfield Parade, Middle Park, Melbourne 3206,
Australia

First published 1977

Printed in Great Britain at the University Press, Cambric

Library of Congress Cataloguing Publication Data

Macfarlane, Alan.
Reconstructing historical communities.

Bibliography:
1. Social history - Methodology. 2. Ethnology -
Methodology. I. Harrison, Sarah, joint author.
II. Jardine, Charles, joint author. III. Title
HN29.M27   301.34'01'8   77-24234

ISBN 0 521 21796 2

CONTENTS

FIGURES

ACKNOWLEDGEMENTS

     The Social Science Research Council have provided two
project grants to support the research partly described in
this book. A Research Fellowship and a grant towards
computing assistance through the Research Centre were both
provided by King's College, Cambridge. I am most grateful
to the Research Council and the Provost and Fellows of
King's College for their indispensable support. Sarah
Harrison undertook most of the very time-consuming research
which lies behind the tables and the discussions in the
book. She also contributed very substantially to the
methodology described here. Charles Jardine's experience in
information processing and retrieval with computers also
played a major part in the developments described below and
he was largely responsible for the final production of the
book in a form which it is estimated will halve its price
to readers. More recently Tim King and Jessica Styles have
made a significant contribution and we have long been
fortunate to have the advice and encouragement of Ken Moody.
Cherry Bryant and Iris Macfarlane have also shared in what
is above all a co-operative enterprise. The Computing
Service in Cambridge and the S.S.R.C. Cambridge Group for
the Study of Population and Social Structure have provided
a great deal of support and expertise. It will be clear that
much of the work was inspired by that of Peter Laslett,

Roger Schofield and Tony Wrigley. My anthropological debts have been listed elsewhere, but I would like to thank my colleagues at the Department of Social Anthropology and particularly Jack Goody for their tolerance of a marginal academic. Many other thanks must go unrecorded, though Dennis Cowan who drew many of the diagrams, and Patricia Williams and Jack Bowles of the Cambridge University Press who helped with the production cannot be overlooked.

My introduction to local records was through the teaching of Hilda Grieve at the Essex Record Office and under the supervision of Keith Thomas. Since then I have incurred a very great debt to the archivists of various record offices, particularly those at Chelmsford, Kendal, Carlisle, Preston and the Public Record Office, London. More specifically, I am grateful to the following archivists for permission to reproduce the plates in the text: Essex (figures 2:3, 2:4, 2:5, 2:6, 2:7, 2:8, 2:9, 2:11, 2:12 and the cover); Lancashire (figure 2:13); Cumbria (figure 2:14). Figure 2:10 is reproduced by permission of the Public Record Office; Crown copyright material is reproduced by permission of the Controller of Her Majesty's Stationery Office.

Alan Macfarlane,
Department of Social Anthropology,
Downing Street, Cambridge

Chapter 1

GENERAL APPROACHES TO THE ANALYSIS OF COMMUNITIES

1:1 The myth of the community.

The belief that stable and tightly-knit communities have existed in the past and still survive in distant lands is an important myth for industrial and highly mobile societies. It is therefore no coincidence that it was in the turmoil of late nineteenth-century industrialization that the idea of 'community' as opposed to modern 'society' was developed extensively, particularly in the work of Tonnies (1887). It was felt that society was changing, values were being undermined, an older closeness was being lost. This powerful myth both influenced, and seemed to find support in, the work of historians and anthropologists during the first half of the twentieth century. Westerners visiting remote areas of the world were able to discern those 'communities' which were already just a memory in their own society. Commenting on Indian villages, for example, the anthropologist Srinivas remarked that 'nobody can fail to be impressed by the isolation and stability of these village communities' (Srinivas 1960: 23). The work of social and economic historians often pointed to a community-based society, later destroyed by industrialization and urbanization. As Tonnies described it, the emphasis in 'community' was on blood (bonds of kinship), place (geographical bonds), and mind (the sentiment of belonging to a group). All these elements, he argued, had been broken in the transition to modern 'society'. Community in this sense could be defined as 'a territorial group of people with a common mode of living striving for common objectives' (Ruth Glass in Frankenberg 1966: 201)

Yet, despite the assumed existence of 'communities', it has been very difficult to define the term more precisely. A recent summary of the contributions of various sociologists to 'community studies' has concluded that the 'concept of community has been the concern of sociologists for more than two hundred years, yet a satisfactory definition of it in sociological terms appears as remote as ever' (Bell & Newby 1971: 21). One survey of the very large literature using the concept of 'community' considered ninety-four different definitions, yet was forced to conclude that 'all of the definitions deal with people. Beyond this common basis, there is no agreement' (Bell & Newby 1971: 27 quoting Hillery). Even this minimum definition is not satisfactory since there are, for example, 'community studies' of animals other than man. Another minimum definition that has been suggested is that 'community implies having something in common' (Frankenberg 1966: 238). This appears to be the original dictionary meaning of the term. Yet, having something in common does not necessarily imply 'community' in any sociological sense of the word. If it did, then all red-headed persons or all suicidal maniacs would be a 'community' and the term would be practically meaningless.

Two recent attempts to discuss the 'myth of community' and the definitional problems associated with it deal with this topic in a way that is not possible here (Stacey 1969; Bell & Newby 1971: ch. 2). One of their major theoretical

steps is to differentiate the geographical and the social
aspects of community studies which had been merged by
Tonnies and Frankenberg in the discussions alluded to above.
Stacey has pointed out that though they may overlap, the social relationships within a defined geographical area are
theoretically distinguishable from the sense of 'belonging
to a group' which such physical proximity is said to entail
(1969: 135). In fact, a 'community', she argues, may be
geographically based or it may not. Furthermore, since sociologists are interested in the social relationships rather
than the geographical space, it may be mistaken to demarcate
the area of interest on the basis of physical space. Stacey
argues that 'our concern as sociologists is with social
relationships. A consideration of the social attributes of
individuals living in a particular geographic area is
therefore not sociology, although it may be an essential
preliminary to sociological analysis' (1969: 136). Or, as
Bell and Newby put it, 'a community study must be concerned
with the study of the interrelationships of social institutions in a locality' (1971: 19).

The second fundamental point made by Bell and Newby is
the distinction between 'community studies' as a method of
study, in other words as a preliminary to further investigation or a way of collecting relevant data, and the community
study in which the 'community' is treated as a theoretical
concept. In the latter case it is assumed that the concept
of 'community' reflects some reality in the observed and external world; that it is a heuristic concept that makes the
phenomena more intelligible. Unfortunately, the two uses
tend to become confused since it is likely that the method
will lead to the collection of data which persuades the
investigator that he really is studying a 'community' in the

second sense outlined above. Despite the confusion, it is
essential to keep in one's mind that ultimately the 'community study' approach can have these two senses. It can
either be the selection of a unit of observation, for example 1,000 persons at one point in time, or the analysis
of a unit which it is believed has some internal structure
which is more than random, in other words a 'system' of some
kind.

1:2 The community study as a method.

The present work is designed as a contribution to the
use of 'community' in the methodological sense, as a means
of collecting and organizing data. It makes no assumptions
about the actual existence or absence of 'communities of
sentiment' or any other kind of community among the objects
of its study. In common with a number of disciplines, it
shares an interest in the methodological usefulness of
taking small, bounded, collections of items, whether human
or non-human, as a convenient focus for analysis. Among the
disciplines interested in this approach, the following may
be selected at random; social anthropology, sociology,
archaeology, history, ethology, ecology, genetics,
demography. These are but a few. The main purpose of listing
them is to stress that it is the general method, rather than
the nature or existence of any supposed 'community' of a
specific kind, which is our principal concern. It should
also be apparent that any general method of community
analysis developed within one discipline will have repercus-
sions on all the others. For example, the development of the
'participant-observation' fieldwork method in British social
anthropology in the early part of the twentieth century came
to influence both sociology and the study of animal

behaviour. Any attempt to devise a general method must
therefore be wide enough to deal with data which is
intrinsically very different from that for which it is
specifically constructed.

A second reason for briefly listing the disciplines
interested in this approach is to stress that the following
discussion, which is centred on the three disciplines with
which we are most familiar, namely social anthropology,
sociology and history, only covers one corner of the field.
Yet, even to survey such an area means a wider spread than
that attempted by whole books devoted to surveying community
studies. For example, the work by Frankenberg only considers
one discipline, sociology, and, within that discipline, one
geographical area, Britain. Bell and Newby widen their scope
to include American and European studies, but still remain
essentially within the discipline of sociology. Neither of
these books attempt to take account of the very considerable
literature on non-western 'communities' produced by social
anthropologists, or on 'past' communities by historians.

1:3 Some criteria for measuring community studies.

The numerous 'community studies' undertaken in Western
Europe and North America have already received considerable
attention in textbooks (Frankenberg 1966; Bell & Newby
1971). To these we might add large numbers of monographs by
social anthropologists on non-western peoples. These range
from the early works on the Trobriands, Tikopia and Nuer,
through studies of villages in the Himalayas, India, Mexico,
New Guinea and elsewhere, to recent studies of Latin
American, African and other 'communities'. There has also
been a tradition of community studies by English historians,
which has recently been revitalized by American, French and

other studies which will be discussed below.

The size of the 'communities' studied by these three disciplines varies considerably. Sociologists tend to take the largest unit. For example, Middletown, studied by the Lynds, grew from 11,000 to 35,000 persons over the period of analysis; Banbury consisted of some 19,000 when it was first studied. Yankee city consisted of over 16,000 persons (Bell & Newby 1971: 85, 181, 106). The figures are misleading, however, for the projects were based on small teams of researchers. Banbury, for example, was studied by a team of three; there were at least 18 persons doing fieldwork on Yankee city, a ratio of less than 1 per 1,000 of the population (Bell & Newby 1971: 101, 106). When only a single investigator is involved, the population is often very small. Gosforth numbered a little over 700 Ashworthy a little over 500, when Williams studied them. About 1,000 to 3,000 per investigator is the norm among social anthropologists. Leach studied about 500 people in depth among the Kachin (Leach 1954: 66); Tikopia contained roughly 1,200 persons when Firth did his early fieldwork (Firth 1939: 41); Pitt-Rivers' Andalusian township contained about 2,000 persons (1954; 4). Such communities are believed to be representative samples within a larger population of, for example, 300,000 Kachin or 200,000 Nuer (Leach 1954: 3; Evans-Pritchard 1940: 110). The size of communities in the past at one point in time is less helpful when considering the works of historians. Obviously, the cross-sectional population needs to be multiplied by the number of years over which the population is studied. Thus, Hoskins studied the Leicestershire parish of Wigston Magna which had an estimated population of about 400 in 1563; but his study covered a period of over nine centuries (Hoskins 1957: 177).

The three communities studied by Spufford contained nearly
2,000 people, but were only analysed in detail for two
centuries (Spufford 1974). The work by Wrigley on the parish
of Colyton was based on between 1,500 and 2,000 persons, but
only one aspect of their lives in the four centuries under
consideration was singled out for analysis, namely the
demographic (Wrigley 1966). The work by Greven on an
American parish covered a population that averaged between
1,000 and 2,000 over a period of about one and a half
centuries (Greven 1970). The general impression one receives
is that the ratio of 1 investigator per 2,000 people or less
is essential in order to undertake really intensive 'community studies' by conventional methods.

As stated above, the number of persons to be studied
has to be interrelated with the temporal *time* dimension of the
study. It is well known that the absence of information
about the past, as well as a certain theoretical framework,
limited early social anthropologists to a study of their
'community' at one point in time. Later in the history of
the discipline there was a growing interest in change and
time. Thus Firth studied Tikopia on a number of visits over
half a century. Land records enabled Kessinger, Leach,
Obeyesekere and others to study economic and social change
in India and Sri Lanka from the middle of the nineteenth
century onwards (Kessinger 1974; Leach 1961; Obeyesekere
1967). Yet it still remains true that most social anthropologists study a society intensively over a period of one
or two years, supplementing this with small amounts of data
on the past.

A good deal of the early work on western societies was
also 'timeless', for example that by Warner and his team,
and by Arensberg and Kimball. But a growing number of

studies included a considerable time depth. The Lynds
studied 'Middletown' in America over the period 1890-1924
and made extensive use of historical records. Williams
studied land ownership and social change in Ashworthy from
the middle of the nineteenth century. Lison-Tolosano
studied Belmonte de los Cabaleros from the sixteenth
century onwards. John Davis' recent study of land and family
in South Italy covers the period 1861-1961 in some depth
(Bell & Newby 1971: 82-91; Williams 1963; Lison-Tolosano
1966; Davis 1973) A hundred years is a long time in sociological or anthropological work, but some historians have
studied communities for much longer periods. Perhaps the
longest is the work by Hoskins on a Leicestershire parish,
which is analysed in some detail from the eleventh to nineteenth centuries (Hoskins 1957). Or again, Spufford
considered certain economic aspects of Chippenham in
Cambridgeshire from the thirteenth to nineteenth centuries
(Spufford 1965).

Six hundred years is not out of the question for a
historian; but as yet there has been no true marriage of the
two modes, sociological and historical. The very intensive
study of daily interactions and everyday thoughts which is
the hallmark of social anthropology and micro-social history
has not been achieved over long time periods. The ex-
planation lies partly in the very nature of the data, but
also in its sheer bulk. It is possible for a single observer
to watch one thousand persons interacting over one year; but
to study these same thousand persons over two hundred years
or more would be impossible. It would be the equivalent of
studying a town of 200,000 at one point in time, a project
which would immediately strike any investigator as
impracticable, even if the data were good enough. There are,

therefore, considerable technical problems to be overcome
before the various social sciences interested in 'communities' in the present and past are able to collaborate
effectively.

The degree to which the 'community' is closed or
bounded both geographically and socially varies from
discipline to discipline. It seemed reasonable to assume,
when studying the small island of Tikopia, or the Trobriand
islands, that there really was some kind of bounded community. The societies visited by the first social anthropologists were often isolated. Their fieldwork methods were
evolved in this context. One of the main theoretical
problems for that discipline and others has been the
transfer of early techniques to situations where there is
no geographical isolation. At first sight the problem might
seem least acute when the methods were applied to communities in the past. Medieval villages, for example, might
seem to fit the criterion of isolation rather better than
modern industrial nations. The concept of an isolated rural
community seemed to be based on reality. Now, we know that
the idea is largely a myth. The very great degree of short-
range geographical mobility in England from at least the
fifteenth century and the interconnectedness of economy and
society from at least the thirteenth century is now well
established, for instance by Postan's work (1973). Any
particular community in England in the past was probably no
more isolated than a Chicago suburb or twentieth century
Banbury. For this reason, the theoretical problems
afflicting modern sociologists and social anthropologists
apply with equal force to historians.

The way in which we locate 'communities', in other
words the indices we employ to measure them, has been a

plural
of index

topic of more concern to sociologists and social anthropologists than to historians. The latter tend to fall back
on some unit of administration such as the parish. Some
suggestions concerning the ways in which a community could
be measured were made by Redfield in his work on the Little
Community. He suggested that they must be distinctive, small
in size, homogenous and economically self-sufficient (1957:
4). By these criteria, many of the so-called 'community
studies' are not studies of communities at all. Elsewhere
Redfield suggests the following indices: frequent interpersonal contacts; wives taken from within the area; group
feeling in political emergencies (1957: 120-1). He supple-
ments these by suggesting as indices, a common name, common
sentiment, the payment of debts within the 'community'
(1957: 118). Again the definitions appear to be either too
blunt to be helpful, or too tight to enable us to study
anything except a completely closed island. A more recent
attempt to list some of the criteria to be used has been
made in a book which applies some anthropological techniques
to a Spanish town. Pitt-Rivers lists some of the reasons
which makes him think that his Andalusian *pueblo* is a 'community'. There is a sentiment of attachment to the *pueblo*
which stems from membership at birth; folklore reflects
pueblo divisions; there are minor dialect boundaries between
pueblos; there are minor differences in material culture,
for example clothing; outsiders are often treated roughly;
ritual and religion is localized, for example there are
local patron saints; reputations are common property within
the *pueblo* and gossip is strong (1954: ch. 1). Pitt-Rivers
concludes that 'the community is not merely a geographical
or political unit, but the unit of society in every context'
(1954: 30-1). It would not be difficult to add indices to

the list. There is the area within which mystical sanctions such as cursing and witchcraft are effective. There is the area within which shame and guilt are felt, the 'moral community' as Campbell describes it (1964: 259, 310). Other major indices are as follows: shared conscious models: areas of economic exchange; areas of joint agricultural activity; the marriage arena; the area for recruitment to rituals; dialect; costume; social treatment of the dead; area for support in various crises; administrative area; field for informal social control; range of gossip and scandal; area within which the prestige hierarchy operates.

If one were fortunate enough to find an area where all these criteria overlapped, it would look something like figure 1:1. Such an overlap has been suggested by Skinner for Chinese 'standard market communities' but unfortunately, for most investigators, many of the indices do not normally overlap symmetrically (Skinner 1964). This is fairly self-evident when we are studying industrialized and urbanized societies, but it may come as a surprise that often there is little overlap even in rural non-western and 'traditional' societies. The situation we tend to find in many cases is that illustrated in figure 1:2. A classic

Figure 1:1. Isolated communities; a few indices: costume, personal networks *etc.* are ommitted.

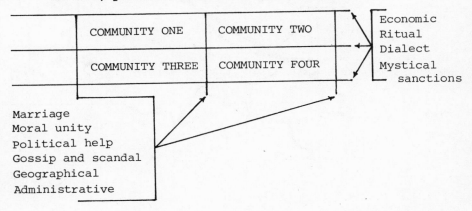

illustration of the lack of overlap in a non-urbanized society is that described for rural Bali by Geertz. Taking seven indices (shared obligation to worship at a given temple, common residence, ownership of rice land lying within a single watershed, commonality of ascribed social status or caste, consanguineal and affinal kinship ties, common membership in one or another 'voluntary' organization, common legal subordination to a single government administrative official) Geertz looked at specific Balinese 'villages'. He found that 'virtually nothing is coordinate with anything else and the crisscrossing of loyalties reaches an almost unbelievable degree of intricacy' (1959: 1001). In other words, those who worshipped together were not the same as those who farmed together; those who farmed together were not the same as those with a common residence;

Figure 1:2. Overlapping communities; for simplicity only a few indices are included.

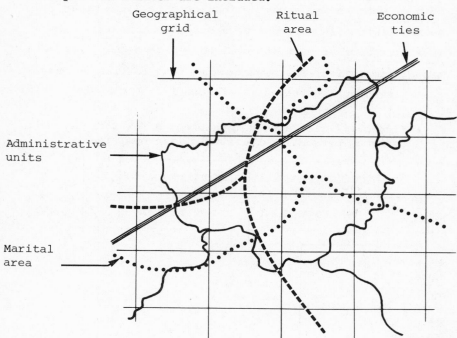

Geographical grid

Ritual area

Economic ties

Administrative units

Marital area

those who lived together were not the same as those with
kinship ties and so on. We are therefore left with an
incredibly complex set of 'planes' which may or may not
overlap. One way of putting the problem on one side is to
talk of the 'economic community' or the 'moral community',
the 'marriage community' or the 'community of gossip'. One
can, in fact, make 'community' into an activity-specific
word.

The difficulties are further compounded by the fact
that there are different 'levels' of community. Redfield
has distinguished three of these; there is the community of
what ought to happen (the moral community); the community
of what is thought does happen; the behavioural or statistical community of what does, if counted, happen (1957:
44-5). As with the various indices which we have discussed
above, these may overlap. People may behave statistically in
the way that they are thought to behave and it is conceived
that they ought to behave. Yet it is often the case that
the three different levels are entirely at variance. This
'anomic' situation, as it is sometimes termed, is likely to
cause confusion in the investigator as well as in the people
who exhibit the conflicting patterns. It is no longer clear
how the analyst is to fit together his informant's ideas
of how people ought to behave alongside the statistical
situation which emerges from counting cases. The conflict
in the observer partly arises from the fact that he is
likely to be collecting two entirely different kinds of
data. The central methodological characteristic of the
'community study' approach appears to be the total
involvement of the researcher in a delimited area, geographical or social. With a ratio of 1 investigator to 1,000
or so, it is possible to get to know most of the members of

of the population under observation and to indulge in the
'participant observation' characteristic of social anthropology. But two other major kinds of material are collected;
statements by informants mainly at the level of what ought
to happen, and the observations, including the counting of
instances, made by the investigator. It is when these
various kinds of information clash, as they often do, that
both the most rewarding and the most difficult work begins.

1:4 Some criticisms of the community study.

While 'community studies' proliferate, objections to
both the concept of 'community' and the methodology have
grown. A number of these criticisms may be stated briefly.
It is argued that such community studies are, in practice,
non-comparable and non-cumulative. They tend to be more like
novels or works of art than the objective products of a
supposedly rigorous 'social science'. Each study has to be
treated on its own merits and sheds little light, it is
held, on other areas. It is further argued that no amount
of such micro-studies will help us to piece together the
macro-structure of the whole society. As Wolf pointed out
some years ago, 'we cannot hope to construct a model of how
the larger society operates by simply adding more community
studies' (1956: 1066). The same criticism was made by
Freedman when he commented on Radcliffe-Brown's influence
on Chinese studies. The latter's belief was that 'from this
patient induction from studies of small social areas would
emerge a picture of the social system of China. Of all the
biases to which the anthropological approach has been
subject this seems to me to be the most grievous. It is the
anthropological fallacy *par excellence*' (Banton 1966: 124).
A third criticism is that the concepts and methods were

developed for the study of communities which were assumed
to be isolatable and geographically located. Such communities may once have existed, but they are seldom found
today. Nor are they easily found in the past records of
western societies. It is frequently pointed out that this
lack of hard boundaries is more widespread than the work of
some early social anthropologists would lead us to believe.

A fourth criticism is that 'communities' tend to lie in
the eye and methodology of the beholder. As Bell and Newby
have pointed out, the participant observation method and
intensive attention to personal interrelations tend to
create in the sociologist's mind, if nowhere else, a sense
of 'community' and integration. He will find community bonds
and community sentiments because he expects to do so. On the
contrary, mass observation techniques of census and
questionnaire tend to overlook interpersonal bonds and
sentiments of 'belongingness'. Consequently, the latter
methodology emphasizes the atomistic, individualistic,
mobile nature of western urban life. If social anthropologists had only used the questionnaire and census in
Tikopia or among the Nuer, while sociologists had lived in
urban areas for a period of years and noted interactions,
it seems likely that our whole picture of the two situations
would have been reversed. A fifth criticism is that, because
the early community studies were by-products of early
structural-functional anthropological analysis, they were
timeless, overintegrated, 'equilibrium models' which took
little account of change or of conflict. Anthropological and
sociological workers, in their attempt to escape from
ethnocentrism, suffered from what Bierstadt has called
'temporocentrism', which he defines as 'the unexamined and
largely unconscious acceptance of one's own lifetime as the

centre of sociological significance, as the focus to which
all other periods of historical time are related' (Bell &
Newby 1971: 63). Although social anthropologists were at
first merely making a virtue of necessity in the absence of
records of the past, this meant that the tools they
developed, which were later applied by sociologists to
western societies, were not adequate to deal with societies
which do have extensive records of the past. The
subjectivity of the whole 'community study' approach was
shown dramatically by the famous case where two
investigators lived in the same town in Mexico at fifteen-
year intervals. They found entirely different 'communities'
because of their differing interests (Foster 1960).

1:5 Attempts to improve the concepts.
    If the old tools appeared to be too cumbersome to deal
with rural Mexico or Bali, it is not surprising that when,
in the 1950s, they were used in studying Indian townships,
Norwegian fishing communities, or the suburbs of London,
such concepts seemed totally inadequate. It was obvious that
even if one wished to study a particular geographical area,
much more flexible indices and concepts were needed. The
difficulties were summed up by Wolf when he wrote that
'Communities which form parts of a complex society can thus
be viewed no longer as self-contained and integrated systems
in their own right. It is more appropriate to view them as
the local termini of a web of group relations' (1956: 1065).
Although he introduced the term 'broker' groups, and his use
of the word 'web' foreshadows the later term 'network', Wolf
was unable to solve the theoretical difficulties. A number
of attempts have subsequently been made to create a more
flexible and subtle set of analytic categories for the study

of highly mobile societies which are still believed to
contain 'communities' of some kind.

One of these attempts was published in 1957 in Turner's
work 'Schism and Continuity in an African Society'. Earlier
discussions of roles and actors, based on an analogy with
drama, were taken further with the concept of the 'extended
case study' or 'social drama'. The latter was defined as 'a
limited area of transparency on the otherwise opaque surface
of regular, uneventful social life. Through it we are
enabled to observe the crucial principles of the social
structure in their operation, and their relative dominance
at successive points in time' (1957: 93). Turner defined the
processes through which a social drama would go as firstly
a breach of regular norm-governed relations; crisis; redres-
sive action; reintegration or recognition of schism (1957:
91-2). Such an approach had been implicitly employed by a
number of anthropologists, but the more explicit discussion
seemed to free social anthropologists so that they could
study minute processes over time rather than merely take a
timeless cross-section. Combined with the 'case-study
method', in which anthropologists were exhorted to gather
material concerning 'a series of connected events to show
how individuals in a particular structure handle the choices
with which they are faced' (Van Velsen 1967: 140), this made
it respectable to analyse individual actions and motiva-
tions. Although there were the dangers of degeneration into
a narrative and literary mode of pure description, the
concentration on a particular event, rather than on a
particular group or larger unit, appeared to make a more
subtle analysis of life in small 'communities' possible.

In practice the focus of the 'social drama' approach
tended to be on crises of various kinds. It was readily

apparent, however, that the method could be generalized to cover a much wider range of 'events', including political processes both formal and informal. One of the most notable attempts to widen the concept was that made in 1963 in an article on the 'Significance of Quasi-Groups'. Mayer pointed out that for the study of highly mobile and 'complex' systems, it is necessary to move away from the earlier emphasis on enduring 'groups' towards the study of what he termed 'quasi-groups', by which he principally meant the 'action-set'. The action-set 'is not a group ... for the basis for membership is specific to each linkage, and there are no rights or obligations relating all those involved' (in Banton 1966: 109). It is, in fact, the 'set' of people who are mobilized in a certain situation. It is not all of a person's potential contacts, but those people who are called on in a particular faction struggle, crisis, or other event. If a number of such 'action-sets' overlap in membership, they begin to form into a more enduring unit which Mayer terms the 'quasi-group' since it lies half way between the entirely temporary action set and the permanent 'group'. These action-sets were often very small and, argued Mayer, centred on a particular individual who brought them into being on a specific occasion. When combined with the 'social drama' approach, sociologists now had better tools for studying much more fluid and complex structures.

Nine years before Mayer presented his paper, Barnes had introduced the concept of 'network', which Frankenberg describes as 'the first *major* advance in the language of sociology since role' (1966: 242). Bell and Newby agree that the concept of network is very important indeed for the future of community studies. They state that 'what little empirical data there is directly relating to social networks

leads us to believe that it is indeed a powerful analytical
tool' (1971: 53). The term and the concept were not entirely
new when used by Barnes. Nor was the need for such an
analytic device concealed. The year before Barnes' seminal
article was published, Redfield gave some lectures on the
Little Community in which he commented on Rees' Welsh study
in the following words. 'The hearth of the lonely farm is
the only center. There is no community centering upon town
or village; there is only a double network of kinship
connection and neighbourly connection to hold together,
loosely, people who dwell separate from one another ...
there are no fixed groups' (1957: 6). Despite this earlier
use, it was only in Barnes' study that the term was given
serious analytic content. During the last twenty years a
very considerable literature on 'network analysis' has grown
up, and some of the major readings are indicated in the
bibliography to this book. A number of definitional and
substantive battles have been fought. This is not the place
to go over this complex ground, but it is important to
sketch in one or two of the landmarks.

The original classic definition by Barnes, when
attempting to analyse his Norwegian community, was as
follows. He isolated three regions or fields in the social
system, the third of which is 'made up up of the ties of
friendship and acquaintance'. He continues that 'each person
has a number of friends, and these friends have their own
friends; some of any one person's friends know each other,
others do not. I find it convenient to talk of a social
field of this kind as a *network*. The image I have is of a
set of points some of which are joined by lines. The points
of the image are people, or sometimes groups, and the lines
indicate which people interact with each other' (1954: 43).

As Frankenberg pointed out, the concept was very similar indeed to that of the 'topological graph' as used by mathematicians and it is perhaps no coincidence that Barnes was a mathematician by training. Later investigators attempted to make further distinctions, principally between the 'general network' of all potential and actual links, and what is sometimes called the 'personal' or 'ego-centred' network on the other. Barnes rejects the latter terms and refers to them as 'stars'. Further elaborations have been made not only to make it possible to differentiate the focus of the network, but also to distinguish degrees of distance from any selected individual in a given 'network'. A growing number of criteria have been suggested as to how interpersonal relations should be measured (interpersonal criteria) and how the overall shape of networks (morphological or structural criteria) should be compared. The 'diversity of linkages', content of linkages, directional flow, frequency of interaction, duration, intensity of interaction, are among the major interactional criteria. Size, density, degree of connection, centrality, and clustering are some of the measures suggested for analysing the structure of networks.

While most sociologists agree that the network concept is extremely powerful, no one has yet found a way of utilizing it properly. The data-gathering and analysis are so arduous that traditional sociological methodology is inadequate. The point has been made by all those who have attempted to undertake a network analysis. For example, Mitchell has commented that the 'study of personal networks requires meticulous and systematic detailed recording of data on social interaction for a fairly large group of people, a feat which few fieldworkers can accomplish successfully' (1969: 10-11). Or again, he writes that 'the characteristics of the personal network must then be abstracted from the field notes. But the interaction is often so complicated that even the most gifted fieldworker stands to miss a good deal. Some systematization of the categories of information to be recorded would obviously improve the quality of the analysis' (1969: 33). Perhaps the most serious attempt to undertake a full network analysis is that by Boissevain. His findings suggest that the approach is extremely difficult in practice. He points out that 'one of the major unresolved problems in the use of networks (is) size. Social anthropologists as yet lack the methodological sophistication needed to tackle this problem' (1974: 71). He further recounts how he 'began with two informants in 1968 on a pilot study basis, planning to branch out and test findings more systematically on a wider sample. Collecting this data proved to be very difficult and very time-consuming, as did its analysis. Hence, for better or for worse, I have data on only two first-order zones' (1974: 97). For example, one informant had 1,750 persons in his 'star' or 'personal network'. Thus to calculate the degree to which they interacted with each other needed a matrix of 1,750 by 1,750. As Boissevain commented, this alone 'reached the memory limits of all but the largest computers' (1974: 36). To gather and analyse the data for the much more intensive type of work suggested by concepts such as 'social drama', 'action-set', 'network' suggests that the organization of sociological and anthropological research will need to be changed. It is perhaps no coincidence that at the very time when the new conceptual tools, some of them derived from mathematics, become widespread, the power to use them has begun to be available in the form of computers.

1:6 Attempts to improve the quality of the data.

The various criticisms made against 'community studies' as well as the growing demands for richer materials in order to test out the conceptual tools outlined in the last section, suggested that data of a new kind was needed. Information on much larger numbers of people over much longer periods of time was required in order to test out hypotheses and to avoid charges of ehistoricity, statistical insignificance and so on. A similar situation occurred within demography, where the need for better data was felt by French demographers in the 1950s. Some of them turned to material from their own nation in the past. In the archives they found data of a quality and duration which they could not obtain from elsewhere. It is therefore not strange if those seeking to improve the quality of anthropological and sociological analysis should turn to past records in order to see if they contain material on interactions of a sufficient quality and quantity. The first section of the book below attempts to see, within a very specific context, to what extent the data does exist. Yet 'data' is not just 'out there' to be harvested, it is not a finite quantity, but rather an organic and infinite growth. Its quantity and quality will depend very considerably on the simple techniques whereby it is collected. It is for this reason that technological developments in data collection, for example in such apparently mechanical things as photography, tape-recording, and computers, will have a very great effect on the very nature of the information that seems to be objectively waiting recovery. One example of perhaps the most ambitious attempt ever made to study a 'community' will

show the way in which a certain methodology subtly
influenced the type of questions which could be asked of the
apparently objective data.

In the 1930s Warner and his associates undertook the
study of Yankee city. This highly ambitious project is well
described by Bell and Newby (1971: 104-6). It was based
above all on the 'Social Personality Card', onto which data
collected by observation, interview and from documents and
newspapers was collated. We are told that 'There was one
card for each adult in the community. On them were recorded,
name, residence, age, sex, social status, occupation, maiden
name of wife, names of children, membership of cliques and
associations, church affiliation, type of house, newspapers
and magazines taken, movies attended, doctor and undertaker
and summary budget data... Also any information from public
welfare and police records relating to each individual was
added. These data were punched on to machine-readable cards
and described statistically' in the five ensuing volumes on
Yankee city. The general aim was a total study; 'the
general objective of our research was to determine the
complete set of social relations which constituted Yankee
City society' (in Bell & Newby 1971: 105). The data,
collected over the years 1930-4, was based on 16,785
individuals. We are told that 'Warner appreciates that the
key problem about his Social Personality Cards is that they
are "data centred on individuals". So whilst they lend
"themselves readily to statistical compilation and correlation of attributes and relational characteristics of
individuals... difficulties arose, however, when it became
necessary to compare one relation between individuals with
another"' (Bell & Newby 1971: 106). The methods of data
collection and data analysis in this colossal study were

obviously crucial. As with the method of gathering fieldwork notes in social anthropology, the method had an enormous influence on the final results.

In social anthropology, there have been various technical developments which have revolutionized the gathering of material since the Second World War. Some of these innovations and their consequences are interestingly set out in a recent work by Chagnon where the use of cameras and computers, as well as more traditional fieldwork methods, are discussed with unusual clarity and in unusual detail (Chagnon 1974). His work, as well as the Yankee city study, emphasize the well recognized point that the collection and subsequent analysis of the data on 'communities' cannot, except at a very theoretical level, be held apart. This is especially so in the case of one of the major tools likely to play a growing part in improving both the quality of the original data and the final results, namely the computer.

1:7 Conclusion.

This brief survey of some of the history of community studies has only touched on a few of the more interesting studies. It is necessarily biased towards certain disciplines and certain problems. It does reveal, that while the 'community study' approach can be criticized on many levels, the method of studying small, delimited, sets of people or other objects is of fundamental interest to many different disciplines. Furthermore, it suggests that some advances could be made if we could find large quantities of good data over long periods of time which were suitable for manual and computerized analysis. The ensuing chapters are a preliminary attempt to argue that such data does exist and

to explain how it is currently being analysed by hand. Of
necessity, this report on a current project cannot serve as
a manual, but it may prove of interest to the considerable
number of people who are involved with historical data, or
the analysis of small groups. It is partly designed to fill
the need expressed after a conference on record linkage.
Laurence Glasco remarked that 'What was lacking, however,
in most of the presentations was a sense of detail that
would allow one to follow the researcher step-by-step
through the solution of a specific problem. It would have
been helpful to be able to follow even one such example,
observing the exact layout of the basic sources (persons
working with census materials have only a vague idea of what
parish records look like, and vice versa), a flow-chart
which would apply to all possible cases one's sources might
present, how the material looked at each intermediate step,
and how inconsistencies were resolved' (Glasco 1971).
Accounts of how to undertake hand analysis of parish
registers have already been provided by Fleury and Henry for
France, and for English censuses and parish registers, by
Wrigley and his collaborators (Fleury & Henry 1956; Wrigley
1966: ch. 4). No satisfactory manual exists for many other
kinds of record.

Chapter 2

THE NATURE OF THE DATA

2:1 Historical records in general.

In the first chapter we reviewed some of the approaches to the analysis of communities. In order to make the discussion more concrete we will now turn to the specific discipline of history and, within that, to a small part of the data, namely that emerging from English historical communities. This is an illustration of a methodology which, it is believed, will apply to other bodies of data of interest to investigators in other disciplines. It was stressed earlier that studies of communities in the past were only one of many types of community study, but that methods developed in one area of 'community studies' are of interest to all those who study bounded units of various kinds.

Massive deposits of records relating to 'communities' in the past exist for most continents. Findings arising from the growing interest in social history, historical demography and economic history, suggest that such records are even more plentiful and extend over longer periods of time than one might, even ten years ago, have imagined. There is no single reference work which describes the local records for civilizations throughout the world, though there is a useful bibliography in Hollingsworth (1969). This is not the place to remedy this omission, nor are we qualified to do so. Yet a short and necessarily impressionistic

account of how English records compare with those for other
countries is needed. The criteria by which we will judge the
records are as follows. We will be considering the records
of a country, or larger area, as a whole, and not the often
exceptionally rich deposits relating to a particular family
or social group. We will primarily be interested in the
records concerning ordinary people, not those for the
wealthy and powerful which often survive even where there
is no other documentation. We will only consider sets of
documents which survive for a hundred years or more at a
stretch, not the occasional exceptional survey or tax
assessment or inquisition. We will only be describing cases
where at least three different types of record, which in
England might mean manor courts, parish registers and wills,
bear on a particular geographical or social area. The method
we will describe requires the overlap of different sources.
Finally, we will only consider the situation before the
middle of the nineteenth century. It should be stressed that
this is a preliminary sketch which omits many areas through
ignorance and probably oversimplifies the position
elsewhere.

By the criteria outlined above, England as a whole
starts to be historically visible from the end of the thirteenth century and continues so until the present. The
Celtic fringe only begins to be documented in detail from
the second half of the seventeenth century. Within Western
Europe as a whole, it would appear that a number of areas
are suitable for the type of analysis we envisage. The
Italian records are particularly impressive for the fourteenth and fifteenth centuries (Herlihy in Wrigley 1973: 47;
Klapisch in Laslett 1972: ch. 10), and those for Spain may
turn out to be very good from the same or slightly later

period (Linz in Lorwin & Price 1972: ch. 5). The records for France have been extensively studied, particularly the excellent parish registers of the seventeenth century and onwards (Goubert 1960; Goubert 1972). The German records, though they seem to start a little later, are immensely detailed in some areas from the seventeenth century (Berkner 1972; Knodel 1970). Similarly, in Sweden the records start a good deal later than those for England but are better when they do begin (Schofield 1974). The records for the Low Countries and Holland are also likely to prove good (Van der Woude in Laslett 1972: ch. 12).

The East European countries have a varied set of records; in Hungary, Serbia, Yugoslavia and elsewhere there are often deposits that go back at least to the seventeenth century (Hammel in Laslett 1972: ch. 14), but those for Russia do not appear to start in comparable detail until the nineteenth century (Kahan in Lorwin & Price 1972: 361). The North American records do not begin until the seventeenth century, but from then are equal in variability to those described below, while the records for certain parts of Canada are superior to English records (Legare *et al.* 1972). South American material in the early period mainly consists of records made by colonial governments, but may turn out to be good (TePaske in Lorwin & Price 1972: ch. 10). Likewise, in Africa it is now becoming clear that there are more historical records than earlier writers imagined, though it would be difficult to argue that they fulfil the criteria listed above before the middle of the nineteenth century.

A major civilization which has produced a vast number of historical records is India. It is clear that many classes of local records exist for parts of India from the

nineteenth century onwards, and these are beginning to be
exploited by historians and social anthropologists (David
Morris in Lorwin & Price 1972: ch. 13; Kessinger 1970;
Kessinger 1974; Kessinger 1976). The Singhalese records are
also detailed from at least the start of the nineteenth
century (Leach 1961; Obeyesekere 1967).

We end this superficial survey by looking at two
particularly intriguing cases. So far, for duration and
multiplicity of sources, it has been difficult to find any
area which matches England. The two main competitors may be
China and Japan.

At present, very little is known concerning the
historical records of Mainland China, yet vast deposits of
genealogies, gazeteers, diaries and other accounts did once
exist and covered about a thousand years. Many must have
been destroyed in the various upheavals and the present
political climate in China makes it impossible to be sure,
but China may prove to be the most richly recorded of all
civilizations. The other possibility is Japan where the long
feudal period from the twelfth to nineteenth century has led
to the amassing of large numbers of records of all kinds
from censuses, genealogies and 'religious investigation
registers' to tax surveys and diaries. These remarkable
collections are widely dispersed and hence difficult to use,
but their potential for demographic and social history is
now widely recognized (Yanamura & Hanley in Lorwin & Price
1972: ch. 13; Hayami & Uchida in Laslett 1972: ch. 18; Hall
1958; Hanley 1974).

It is particularly difficult to undertake a survey of
the existence of records throughout the world since it is
frequently the case that the documents are not known to have
survived until interest is shown in the possibility of their

existence. In general it is true that the same combination
of circumstances that lead to an archival revolution in
England and Western Europe is affecting societies throughout
the world. The result of these changes is that it has become
clear that archives exist to be analysed for some parts of
the world from before the fifteenth century, that in most
of Western Europe and North America such records exist from
the seventeenth century and for India and Russia from the
nineteenth century. The number of records is beyond computa-
tion. A general method for extracting the maximum amount of
information from them is needed. Thus, while this book is
particularly concerned with English records for the fifteenth to eighteenth century, it is believed that comparable
analyses could be carried out in many other parts of the
world.

The records of English communities start effectively in
the thirteenth century. It is from that century that the
first major source which bears on particular communities
year by year, namely manorial records, commences (Elton
1969: 129-30). Before that date, if we are interested in the
local community, it is impossible to catch more than
unconnected glimpses of individuals. For three centuries
from the thirteenth the records produced by the manorial
administration provide almost all the information we have
for activity at the local level. The sixteenth century
witnessed an explosion of documentation. From the middle of
that century it is possible to combine many different
sources in such a way that we are able to gain a three-
dimensional picture of particular individuals and particular
communities. Specific classes of document emerge and then
disappear and records vary enormously from county to county
and even village to village, yet the following assertions

seem plausible. Firstly, very extensive records exist for many parishes in England from the mid sixteenth century up to the present. Secondly, in some respects, the records are better for the late sixteenth and seventeenth centuries than for any subsequent period, including the recent past. Thirdly, although the records for a parish during the nineteenth century appear different from those for the same community some two centuries before, they are similar in intention and in structure. For example, both sets deal with land ownership, demographic events, disputes, administration of the church and the poor rate. Fourthly, although the survival of records varies from village to village and region to region, the problems and techniques of analysis are uniform. Although the legal differences between different areas need to be understood, whether between the see of York and Canterbury in testamentary dispositions, or between manor and manor in the transfer of customary land, needs to be understood, the records are basically the same in structure from region to region.

If the largely undocumented assertions stated above are true, it would seem fair to sample from the immense records of a nation which, even at the end of the thirteenth century, comprised several million inhabitants. The following discussion will largely be based on the records for only two English counties, Essex and Cumbria. Within those counties only the records for two parishes are examined in detail. Within those parishes only the period 1500–1750 is covered in any depth. Preliminary comparisons with earlier and later periods and with studies made of other villages in other counties, suggest that the techniques are applicable to eighteenth- or nineteenth-century material and to any other English county where records survive.

2:2 Problems in delimiting the study.

Boundaries are necessary but always, to some extent, arbitrary. The analysis of a spatially delimited area is, as we have seen, subject to many criticisms. Yet there is one consideration which explains why so many disciplines have used the 'community study' approach. This is the belief that one should attempt to study the 'totality' of human life, the interconnections and complexities which seem to emerge most fully within a small geographical area. Yet even the most ardent devotees of this method will be aware that it is only a tool; the approach contributes some answers to some questions. Without such a method many of the major problems asked by social scientists cannot be solved. Yet such an approach is unlikely, on its own, to contribute a full answer to any one question. The most important findings are always presented by subject, for example studies of myth, magic, capitalism, slavery, the family, or numerous other general themes. One layer of evidence, however, will come from community studies. Without this dimension, the infinite complexity of evidence from a demarcated area, we are left with an impoverished picture of man. Fully aware of the dangers and limitations of this method, yet resolved to delimit the use of of the voluminous records to a specific area and a specific period, we face the problem of choosing the sample.

A demographer or sociologist might try to choose a 'random sample' of the population using the appropriate statistical techniques. Other disciplines, with defective information at their disposal, are forced to select on the basis of less scientific criteria. Social anthropologists, for example, tend to let practical considerations of distance and terrain weigh heavily while historians searching for a community to study intensively are likely to be influenced by the nature of the surviving records as well as more idiosyncratic criteria such as the distance from their place of residence. In each of these disciplines, as we saw in the last chapter, it has been found convenient for any 'total' study to select an area that holds not more than 2,000 individuals at any one time. The obvious unit for an English or French historian is the parish or group of parishes. This was the unit of ecclesiastical and civil administration for many purposes and hence many of the records with which the investigator will be dealing come to him organized on the parish basis. Manorial jurisdictions often cut across the parish, but can usually be subsumed within a study based on parish boundaries. It will often be necessary to move outside the particular parish in order to follow individuals through their lives or to study a group of parishes in order to obtain a large enough sample. Yet the core of the study will probably be this unit.

The degree of usefulness of a community study will often depend very considerably on the original choice of area. It is therefore worth stating some rather obvious yet basic points concerning such a choice. There are many criteria which affect a decision as to the size and location of the community to be studied. Among these are the type of problem to be studied, the availability of time and money, the availability of documents. There are now some guidelines as to the type of community one should select when undertaking historical demography and these seem a reasonable start for the more general approach suggested here (Wrigley 1966: 104-6). A parish of not less than 800

persons and not more than 1,500 is ideal for many purposes.
Anything smaller than this makes it difficult to assemble
meaningful statistics, anything larger becomes unmanageable
unless one is interested in only one problem or a limited
source. In order to obtain some idea of change a period of
at least a hundred years needs to be studied, even if most
of one's attention is concentrated on a shorter period.

It is clearly necessary to choose a community with as
complete a series of major records as possible and these
records need to be appropriate for the investigator's
particular interests. If detailed work on household
budgeting or agricultural economics is to be attempted,
there must be probate inventories; if crime in the local
area is of central interest, the Quarter Sessions and Assize
records must survive for the period under investigation.
Although it is a considerable oversimplification, it could
be argued that for any study of a local area in England in
the period up to 1841 an area should be chosen which has at
least six out of eight of the following major sources for
a substantial proportion of the period under study: parish
registers, wills, inventories, manorial or other surveys,
manor court rolls, ecclesiastical court records, Quarter
Sessions Records, deeds. If one were particularly interested
in the eighteenth or nineteenth centuries the checklist
would have to be modified.

If the two criteria of size and survival of critical
documents are applied, the prospective investigator will
have his choice narrowed down to certain English counties
and certain parishes within these counties. Less than one
quarter of the total of parishes will be left to choose
from. The final choice of a particular community can be made
on the basis of finding what may be termed a special source.

For example, the parish of Earls Colne in Essex whose
records will be used to illustrate this volume was chosen
because one of the inhabitants kept a most detailed diary
during the seventeenth century. As well as this unique
source there is an unusually good Elizabethan map. Such
'special sources' are not as rare as one might imagine.
There are quite large numbers of parishes with a
particularly good set of court rolls, a listing of
inhabitants before the nineteenth century, an early map. It
is clearly far better to choose a well documented parish or
set of parishes, even though they cannot be proved to be
typical, than to choose a 'random' but poorly documented and
uninteresting place.

2:3 *The convergence of records.*

As Marc Bloch noted, 'the deeper the research, the more
the light of the evidence must converge from sources of many
different kinds' (1954: 67). The basic aim of the approach
adopted here is to gather together and analyse all the
records which relate to a certain set of invididuals in the
past. One strategy is to delimit this set to those who
happened to live at some time in a specific area. In order
to do this the records of nearby areas will also have to be
searched. The very great collections of records generated
at the national level, which are deposited in the central
archives and bear on the selected individuals, will need to
be examined. The approach dictates that every single document concerning the selected area and individuals must be
transcribed or copied in full. It will be shown that the
effect of bringing in further records is not merely addi-
tive; each extra record illuminates all the previously
assembled ones. To omit or abbreviate records because, at

one point of time, they appear to have no great significance
is the counsel of practicality. In the long term, however,
it is folly. Time and man's negligence have selectively
destroyed very large parts of the past; other parts were
never committed to paper. What remains is infinitely pre-
cious and each tiny shred needs to be carefully used.

The reason why one should wish to use all the records
has been alluded to on various occasions. We are interested
in human beings and their activities in as many contexts as
possible. We shall see that the data about the English past
is of such a quality that it is possible to build up
profiles of specific individuals which are, in many
respects, as full as those which we could construct for
living individuals. The essence of the approach is the
necessity that several different records bear on a
particular individual at different points in his or her
life. This concept will be familiar to those who have
studied the 'family reconstitution' technique which links
births, marriages and deaths together in order to build up
demographic profiles of specific individuals. Extended to
incorporate the tens, and often hundreds of other references
to individuals, this approach is the basis of the method
outlined below. An attempt is being made to practice
'individual reconstitution', using every record which
survives for selected individuals. The intellectual rewards
already gained by 'family reconstitution' are well known,
yet they are only a fraction of the rewards to be obtained
from 'total reconstitution'. But just as the returns are
greater with the total approach, so the investment in time
and labour is far greater.

2:4 An inventory of some major records.

France is justly noted for its great regional histories
and for intensive demographic studies of particular
parishes. England on the other hand appears to have one of
the most thriving traditions of local history. There are now
innumerable 'village studies' of particular communities and
many of these illustrate clearly what documents are
available and some of the uses to which they may be put.
Among the best older style parish histories are those by
Cowper (1899), Horsfall Turner (1893), Lucas (1931),
Millican (1937), Pearson (1930), Rushton and Witney (1934),
examples of more recent studies are Hey (1974), Hoskins
(1957), Parker (1976), Spufford (1974). This thriving branch
of history has, since the last war, produced a growing
number of guides to documents. These show, frequently with
extracts from records, what the sources consist of, where
they are to be found, and how they may be used. The best
bibliographical guide to the sources for local history is
Stephens (1973), which may be supplemented by the earlier
guides by Hoskins (1959, 1970). Those who are interested in
carrying out a parish study will naturally refer to these
and other guides. None of these provide a simple checklist
of the major records one might expect to find relating to
an English parish in the past. It would therefore seem helpful to produce such a list, fully recognizing that it cannot
be exhaustive and that no particular parish will have all
these records: see figure 2:1. The other purpose of
producing this brief inventory is to give some idea of the
wealth of historical records relating to English communities
in the past. In the following sections of this chapter we
will merely be selecting twelve major types of document out
of this inventory. It is only fair to point out, however,

Figure 2:1. A selection of major sources for the study of a community. (Starred items are illustrated below)

Individual

Private	Autobiographies, Diaries, Letters
	Business accounts
	Antiquarian collections
	Listings of inhabitants*
Public	General descriptions and tours
	Literary works

Parish

Church	Registers of baptisms *etc.**
	Glebe terriers, Tythe awards
	Churchwarden's accounts
	Vestry minutes
Chapel	Registers of baptisms *etc.*
	Minute books, Account books
Poor Law	Officer's accounts
School	Log books
	Governor's minute books
Monastery	Cartularies
	Accounts
Constables	Accounts
	Settlement orders
	Apprenticeship indentures

Manor

Courts	Books and rolls**
	Views of frankpledge*
Administration	Steward's accounts
	Rentals*
	Surveys, Maps

Borough

Corporation	Journals and order books
	Treasurer's accounts
Courts	Sessions order books and rolls
Trade	Toll books and accounts
Guild	Ordinances
	Minute books, Account books
	Freemen's rolls or books
	Apprenticeship indentures

Figure 2:1 continued.

County

Courts,	Order books
quarter	Rolls
petty	Minute books
hundred	Accounts

Lieutenancy | Muster rolls and books

Administration | Ledgers, Bills and Vouchers
Poll books
Enclosure papers and awards
Registers of electors
Plans of public schemes
Minutes of committees

Ad hoc, | Minute books
Turnpike | Accounts
Canal | Maps

Industry | Company papers

deanery, Archdeanery, | *Bishopric, Archbishopric*
Probate | Wills,* Bonds, Inventories*

Marital | Licences, Bonds *etc.*

Correction | Presentments,* Books

Causes | Depositions, Process books

Clergy | Institutions, Subscriptions

Finance | Fee books, Terriers

Visitations | Books, Licences

Parliament

Lords | Journal
Protestation returns
Petitions, Private bills

Commons | Journal
Public and private acts
Committee papers

Central: Administration

Chancery | Inquisitions *post mortem*
Charter rolls, Patent rolls
Close rolls, Fine rolls

Other | Nineteenth-century census
State papers Domestic
Privy Council register

Figure 2:1 continued.

Central: Financial

Exchequer	Lay subsidies
	Poll tax returns
	Hearth tax returns*
	Inquisitions *post mortem*
Chancery	Inquisitions *post mortem*
Treasury	Papers

Central: Common law

King's Bench	*Coram rege* rolls
	Ancient indictments
Common pleas	Plea rolls
	Feet of fines
	Notes of fines
Assises	Indictments
	Depositions
	Gaol books

Central: Equity

Chancery	Proceedings
	Depositions
Exchequer	Bills and answers

Central: Prerogative

Courts of:	Proceedings, Depositions
Requests	Bills and answers *etc.*
Star Chamber	
Wards and liveries	
General Surveyors	
Augmentations	
First fruits and Tenths	
High Commission	
Council of the North	
Council of Wales and the Marches	

Secondary

Victoria County History
Reference works
Newspapers
Historical Monuments
    Commission reports
Guides to local records

that in terms of sheer volume, these twelve are likely to
contain over two-thirds of the material relating to any
given parish over the period 1500-1841.

2:5 *Twelve specific classes of data.*

The records we shall use to illustrate our approach are
taken from two English parishes during the period from the
sixteenth to nineteenth centuries. One is Earls Colne, near
Colchester, in Essex, with an approximate population of
1,200 in the middle of the period, the other is Kirkby
Lonsdale in Cumbria, with a late seventeenth-century population of about 2,500. The specific records chosen are
believed to be representative of classes of data which can
be found in many different societies at different points in
time. Since this may at first sight seem difficult to
believe, it is worth suggesting, in a very concentrated and
oversimplified way, some of the major disciplines which have
conventionally been interested in such classes of record and
often produced their own data of these types. The main features can be illustrated most simply by a figure: see figure
2:2.

It will be obvious that the allocation of disciplinary
interests is, to a large extent, arbitrary and overlapping.
Most of the disciplines, and others not mentioned, are
interested in most of the types of information listed above.
The table is useful, however, since it shows that, although
the particular records are drawn from the past and have been
traditionally the preserve of local historians, they are
likely to be of much wider interest. This can be illustrated
in greater detail if we take each in turn.

Figure 2:2. Twelve sample records

Class of data	specific record selected for detailed study here	some of the disciplines interested
vital registration	Anglican parish register	demography, physical anthropology
property survey	manorial rental	economic history, sociology, anthropology
property transfer	court baron land transfer	as above and agricultural economics
list of residents	view of frankpledge	anthropology, historical geography
neighbourly relations	court leet case	sociology, social history, anthropology
control of morals	church court case	sociology, anthropology, religious history
criminal action	case at Quarter Sessions	historical criminology, sociology
criminal deposition	Assize deposition	legal history, historical criminology
taxation records	Hearth Tax record	economic and social history, sociology
testamentary bequest	will	social and economic history, anthropology
inventory of goods	probate inventory	economic history, historical geography
list of inhabitants	listing of 1696	demography, sociology, historical geography

2:6 Parish register.

Vital registration information for communities in the
past is contained in many classes of record, among them the
registers of baptisms, marriages and burials of the Anglican
Church. In theory, these registers commence for all English
parishes in 1538 and are replaced by Civil Registration in
1837. In practice, many parishes in England do not have
registers for the first few years, but a large number
commence some time in the sixteenth century. These registers
have been very extensively used during the last fifteen
years, especially by those interested in historical
demography who wish to work out sophisticated measures of
fertility, nuptiality and mortality. The conventions
concerning how to use such documents are well described and
their value is widely appreciated. The methodology is based
on the work of Henry, Fleury, Goubert and other French
demographers and is best described for English readers by
Eversley and Wrigley (Wrigley 1966: chs. 3, 4). One example
of their format, both in the original and after direct
transcription, may be taken from the seventeenth-century
register of Earls Colne in Essex: see figure 2:3. If we
combine the burial register with the other registers of
baptisms and marriages, it is possible to work out very
precise mortality rates, specifying age, sex, marital status
and other variables. Earls Colne with its population of
about 1,200 at the time the document above was produced,
would witness an average of between 20 and 25 burials a
year. Marriage and baptism registers also exist and each
entry in them contains an average of 2 names, for example
a child and a parent or a man and his bride. We would expect
to find about 100 names recorded each year, on average, in
this parish register. These registers exist, with some small

Figure 2:3. An Essex parish register.

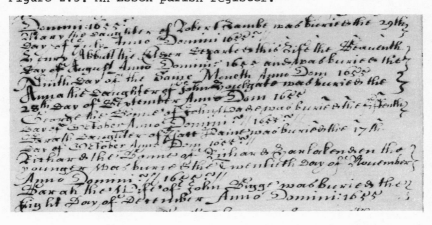

Mary the daughter of Robert Lambe was buried the 29th
day of July Anno Domini 1655

Henry Abbutt the Elder departed this Life the Seaventh
day of August Anno Domini 1655 and was buried the
Ninth day of the Same Moneth Anno Dom 1655

Anna the daughter of John Houlgate was buried the
28th day of September Anno Dom 1655

George the Sonne of John Wade was buried the fifteenth
day of October Anno Domini 1655

Sara the daughter of Isaac Paine was buried the 17th
day of October Anno Dom 1655

Richard the Sonne of Richard Harlakenden the
younger was buried the Twentieth day of November
Anno Domini 1655

Sarah the Wife of John Sigge was buried the
Eight day of December Anno Domini 1655

gaps, from 1558. If we continue until the mid nineteenth
century (using Civil Registers for the last few years), and
count each occurrence of each name as one, we will have
accumulated roughly 30,000 very brief references to
individuals. To extract each entry and then link it up with
other entries relating to the same person (family
reconstitution), would take approximately 1,500 man-hours,
or one year working 30 hours a week, 50 weeks a year.
Wrigley states that, very roughly, to reconstitute a parish
of 1,000 persons for three centuries might take 1,500 hours
(Wrigley 1966: 97). Parish registers are only one of many
sources bearing on mortality; for example, wills and
manorial records often give explicit or implicit information
about people's deaths. Bringing in other records also
enriches mortality statistics very greatly by providing the
social and economic context within which deaths occur.

2:7 Manorial rental.

There is massive documentation of property holding in
England from at least the thirteenth century onwards. The
most voluminous records of ownership are those produced by
manorial officials. The two major classes of manorial
records are the periodic surveys and rentals at specific
points in time, and the continuing registration of transfers
of land and other property in the manor court rolls. Rentals
and surveys exist in large quantities from the fourteenth
to the nineteenth centuries and are sometimes accompanied
by maps. These descriptions of property ownership often
enable one to piece together landholding patterns in
particular parishes every 20 or 30 years. For example,
during the period 1395-1677 there are 14 surviving rentals
of one kind or another for the manor of Earls Colne, or an

average of one every 20 years. Their accessibility and
detailed nature has meant that they have been frequently
used and described by historians. An extract from one such
rental, made in 1638, will give some indication of their nature: see figure 2:4. This is a moderately informative
example of the class; some of the others are much more
detailed, giving the names of previous owners, the measure-
ments of the property, the names of adjoining properties and
their owners. Roughly speaking, each rental contains
descriptions of some 300 pieces of immovable property. Thus
there would be roughly 5,000 small descriptions in the
rentals for Earls Colne up to 1677. Rentals and surveys
continue in abundance until the end of the nineteenth
century, so that a total of 7,000 such individual descriptions for the whole period would not seem excessive. Earls
Colne manor covered slightly over half the parish of Earls
Colne, but only represents approximately half the total
documentation on landholdings since the other manor, Colne
Priory, held considerable lands outside the parish. If we
combine the rentals, even allowing for slightly worse
documentation for Colne Priory, a rough estimate of 12,000
descriptions up to the end of the nineteenth century would
seem likely.

Given the very large number of detailed descriptions,
it is not surprising that even those who are most impressed
by their value should not have been able to make full use
of this class of document. (Spufford 1974: 126n). Yet
England is less well served in this respect than parts of
France with its superb series of land surveys. In terms of
the information they contain, each record is probably
equivalent to two or three parish register entries. Judged
solely by quantity, therefore, this class is roughly equiva-

Figure 2:4. A manorial rental.

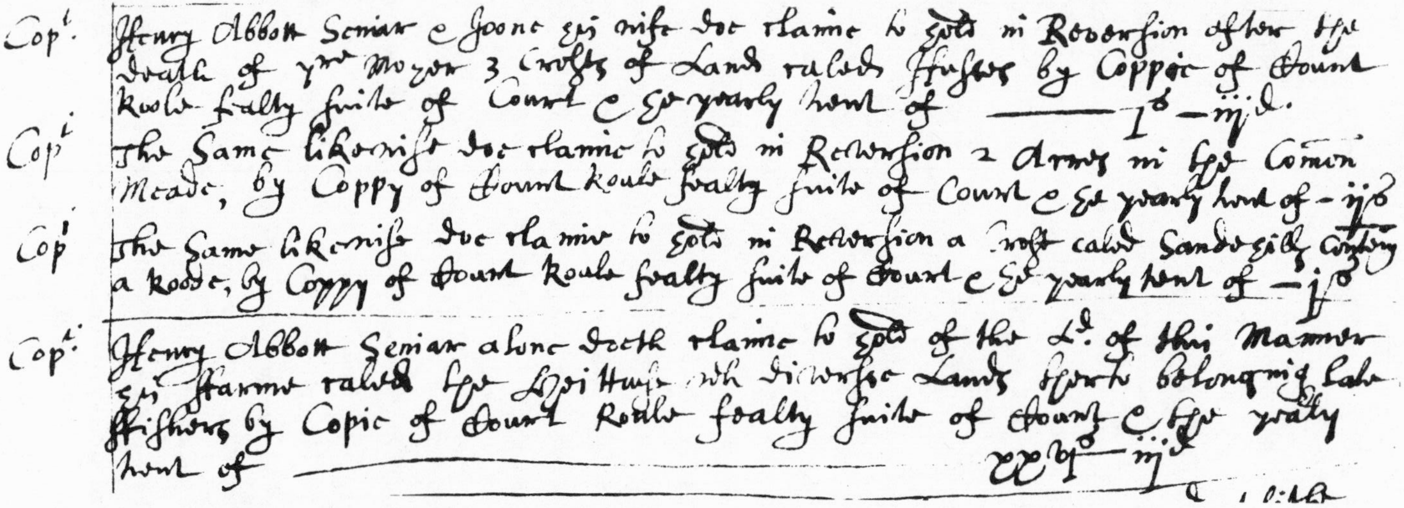

Copi.   Henry Abbott Seniar & Joone his wife doe claime to hold in Reversion after the
death of yre Mother 3 Crofts of land caled Husses by Coppie of Court
Roole fealty suite of Court & the yearly rent of ------ls-iiid

Copi.   The Same likewise doe claime to hold in Reversion 2 Acres in the Common
Meade, by Coppy of Court Roule fealty suite of Court & the yearly rent of -iis

Copi.   The Same likewise doe claime to hold in Reversion a Croft caled Sandehills Containing
a Roode, by Coppy of Court Roule fealty suite of Court & the yearly rent of -js

Copi.   Henry Abbott Seniar alone doeth claime to hold of the Ld. of this Manner
his Farme caled the Hei House with diversse Lands thereto belonging late
Fishers by Copie of Court Roule fealty suite of Court & the yearly
rent of ----------------------------------- xxvis-iijd

lent to the parish registers. Obviously the kind of information is very different from that in the Anglican registers.
Furthermore, it has to be treated with extreme caution. The
rentals cannot be trusted as an index of overall property
holding for many people held land in a number of manors.
There was also a great deal of subletting which is
frequently invisible in rentals. Furthermore, the rentals
normally record owners rather than occupiers and it is
extremely difficult to be sure where a person is actually
living. Despite these difficulties these periodic rentals
and maps do provide the basis for geographical and economic
analysis of communities in the past, as well as providing
a great deal of incidental information on social relationships.

2:8 *Manor court transfer.*

The second major property record is the manor court
roll in which the transfers of certain classes of property
were written down. These documents have been extensively
used by English medieval historians, partly because they are
one of the few sources for local studies in that period.
They are thought to have declined in quality during the sixteenth century and for this and other reasons have been
little used by historians of later periods. Yet in many
parts of England they continue to register land and other
property transfers with almost unabated vigour into the
eighteenth century. Their uses and nature have been
described in a number of studies (Elton 1969: 128-34;
Stephens 1973: 42) One example of a property transfer from
this most voluminous of community records may be given: see
figure 2:5. In our sample parish of Earls Colne, manor court
rolls exist from 1400 to 1931 for the manor of Earls Colne,

Figure 2:5. A manor court transfer.

Figure 2:5 continued. (All but the surnames are translated from the latin)

Court Baron of the said Richard Harlakenden esq. held
Thursday 5th December James by the grace of God of England
France and Ireland King 14 Scotland 50 Anno Dimini 1616
by John Stephens esq. steward

John Read	John Middleton	Robert Rooks
John Pierson	Richard Ward	John Prentice
John Newton	John Parker	Thomas Leffingwell
Nicholas Pierce sworn	Thomas Aylett sworn	Daniel Lea sworn
Richard Parker	Henry Stamer	Israel Ennews
John Hammond	Robt Crowe	Robert Davie
	Clemens Coney	

At the view with court here held on Tuesday the twenty-second of June in the reign of Elizabeth
by the grace of God of England France Ireland late queen defender of the faith &c ten, Henry
Abbott was admitted to one Tenement with two crofts of land containing by estimation two acres
and a Garden adjoining situate in Church street in Colne aforesaid to hold to himself and his
heirs in perpetuity of the lord by the rod &c as by the Roll of this court here brought forward
and shown plainly appears Now at this Court it is found by the Homage that the aforesaid Henry
Abbott died before this Court thus seized And that Henry Abbott his nephew is the nearest heir
of the aforesaid Henry and has the right to the aforesaid premises After which to this Court
came the aforesaid Henry Abbott in his own person and humbly petitions of the lord to be
admitted to the aforesaid premises Wherefore the lord by the hands of his Steward aforesaid
conceded then the right to have to hold and to enjoy the aforesaid Tenement two Crofts of land
and a garden to the said Henry Abbott his heirs and assigns in perpetuity of the lord by the
rod to the will of the lord according to the custom of the manor by rents and services thence
formerly owed and by right accostomed and gave the lord fine and made fealty and is admitted

and for the period from 1489 to 1931 for the manor of Colne
Priory. Allowing for some gaps caused by loss of documents
and counting the manors separately, there are rolls for
about seven hundred years. There are an average of about 10
transfers a year in the Earls Colne rolls and about 5 a year
in those for Colne Priory. A rough estimate would be that
between 5,000 and 7,000 transfers are recorded for this
parish in these rolls. An average of between four and six
persons are referred to in each transfer so that the total
of names alone is roughly similar to the 30,000 estimated
for the parish register. But it will be seen that the
incidental information about relationships and about
property is very much more complex than that in parish
registers. The sheer bulk of information makes them almost
impossible to use. Maitland, one of the greatest authorities
on this source, recognized the difficulty of using them
while also emphasizing their very great value. He wrote,
'How best to garner the great mass of information contained
in the manorial rolls so as to render it available for stu-
dents of legal history is a great question ... A few sets
of rolls completely printed beginning in the thirteenth and
ending in, let us say, the sixteenth century, would be of
inestimable value, especially if they began with surveys or
"extents" and ended with maps' (1889: xi).

Manor court rolls not only give far more detailed
information about the ownership of land and houses than any
other source, they also provide invaluable demographic and
social data. They often fill in family relationships, give
death dates, highlight neighbourly and other bonds. If a
method could be developed to use them in the ways which
Maitland envisaged they should be used, a new dimension
could be added to economic and social history. Yet, as can

be seen from the illustration, they are complicated and
sometimes ambiguous. To understand them and use them
requires considerable knowledge of the legal background
within which they were created.

2:9 View of frankpledge.

Property registration of the kind illustrated above was
the concern of only one part of the manorial jurisdiction,
the 'court baron' as it was known. In theory, the law-
enforcement side of the manorial administration was entirely
separate and was known as the 'court leet' with 'view of
frankpledge'. It was an added prerogative which might or
might not have been granted by the king to a particular
tenant in chief. For this reason, not all villages which
have manors have court leet records. Even those that do have
such records do not always have extensive lists of those who
were sworn into 'frankpledge' or 'views of frankpledge'.
Where such views were held they can be an invaluable source
for the social and demographic investigator (Stephens 1973:
42-3). In theory, they list all the owners and inhabitants
over a certain age who lived within the jurisdiction of the
leet. If people made excuses for not appearing ('essoin')
or defaulted, in other words did not appear, their names
were also recorded. A view for one of the Earls Colne manors
will illustrate their nature: see figure 2:6. It is clear
from this example that although the document does not
provide a great deal of information about individuals, very
large numbers of names appear. Once we know exactly who did
and did not appear, this class of record could provide
important information in our attempt to build up a picture
of individuals in the past. Since they are so detailed, it
is perhaps surprising that they never seem to have been used

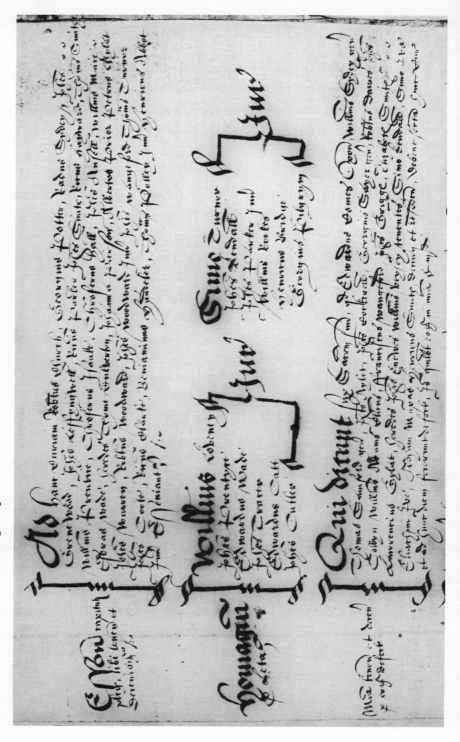

Figure 2:6. A view of frankpledge.

Figure 2:6 continued. (All but the surnames are translated from the latin)

At this Court Robert Church, George Potter, Ralph Sydey, John GreneWood, John Leffingwell, Richard Parker, John Smith, Richard Haywood, Thomas Smith

Essoined Chief William Prentice, Christopher Isaake, Christopher Hall, John Ansell, William Marce
pledges free Esdrs Wade, heirs of Thomas Culverton, Joan Pierson, Albery Prior, Peter Gylat,
tenants & John Warren, Robert Woodward, John Woodward jun., John Wangeford, Thomas Turnor,
deceners John Coote, Richard Clarke, Benjamin Handeler, Thos Polley jun., Henry Abbott
jun. were essoined

William Loveney	Simon Turner	
John Prentyce	John Kendall	
Edward Wade	Jury	John Parker jun.	Jury
John Tracer	William Rookes	
Edward Catt	Henry Bridge	
John Cutler	George Pilgrim	

Homage
for Leet

Tenants & Who said on their oath that Edward Earl of Oxford, William Sydey gent, Thomas
deciners in Samford gent, John Aylet, John Cockerell, George Sayer gent, Robert Dawes, John
mercy for Collyn, William Adams cleric, Francis Wangeford, John Grigges, Elizabeth Smith,
default Lawrence Gylat, heirs of John Enews, William Veysey tenants, Simon Kendall, Simon
Ive, Eliochim Ive, Adham Mapas, Henry Smith deceners and residents, owe suit at
this court and on this day made default, therefore each of them is in mercy iiid

very extensively by historians. Once again, it is probably the practical problem of size which is largely responsible. The views were supposed to be held and recorded twice a year. In practice, in Earls Colne, they seem to have been recorded about once a year. In the manor of Earls Colne there are such views over most of the period 1400-1700 and in Colne Priory manor sporadically between 1490 and about 1700. When a view was held, between 50 and 100 names were usually recorded. Allowing for the loss of records, this parish produced roughly between 20,000 and 30,000 names in the views of frankpledge up to the end of the seventeenth century. Again, this is comparable to the whole parish register and the problem of linking in these names is clearly formidable.

2:10 Court leet.

The 'view of frankpledge' was part of the general peace-keeping machinery delegated to certain lords. Those appearing had to take an oath that they would keep the peace and abide by the customs of the manor. Those who did not abide by their oath could be presented at the 'court leet', a judicial court which had competence to deal with petty crime. Since the 'court baron' also had jurisdiction in certain not totally dissimilar matters, and the records are written together on the same parchment roll, it is often difficult to separate the cases. The nature of these records can be illustrated by a short set of presentments in the Earls Colne manor court against one individual: see figure 2:7. It will be seen that such cases can provide us with material on interpersonal relations which give flesh to the economic and demographic records which we have previously been describing. It is therefore again somewhat surprising

that they have been so little used by historians of the
early modern period in England. As with other manorial
records, part of the problem seems to be sheer size. In
Earls Colne, the court leet remained active until the end
of the first quarter of the seventeenth century. On average,
between 20 and 30 cases a year were presented in the two
courts combined. Allowing for the loss of a good number of
original court rolls, it would seem reasonable to estimate
that between 3,000 and 4,000 court leet cases of one kind
or another survive for this parish, mainly in the period to
1620. Although less in size and complexity than the records
previously discussed, they still constitute a large amount
of data. Preliminary work suggests that court leet records
are available for a good number of English parishes in the
period up to the middle of the seventeenth century.

   2:11 Ecclesiastical court.
   There were numerous other courts with jurisdictions
which complemented that of the court leet. Those which were
most similar in their detailed supervision of village
behaviour were the various church courts. It was believed
by many in England until at least the middle of the seventeenth century that the Anglican Church had the right to
supervise morals, for example to control sexual, marital and
other affairs. The records of the ecclesiastical courts are
therefore a valuable source for the study of topics such as
social control, the nature of interpersonal tensions, sexual
misdemeanours, witchcraft and sorcery. There were many
levels of court, but the one with the most extensive records
in the county of Essex is that of the Archdeacon. These
archdeaconry records, as well as those of the other
ecclesiastical courts, have been widely described and we now

Figure 2:7. A court leet presentment.

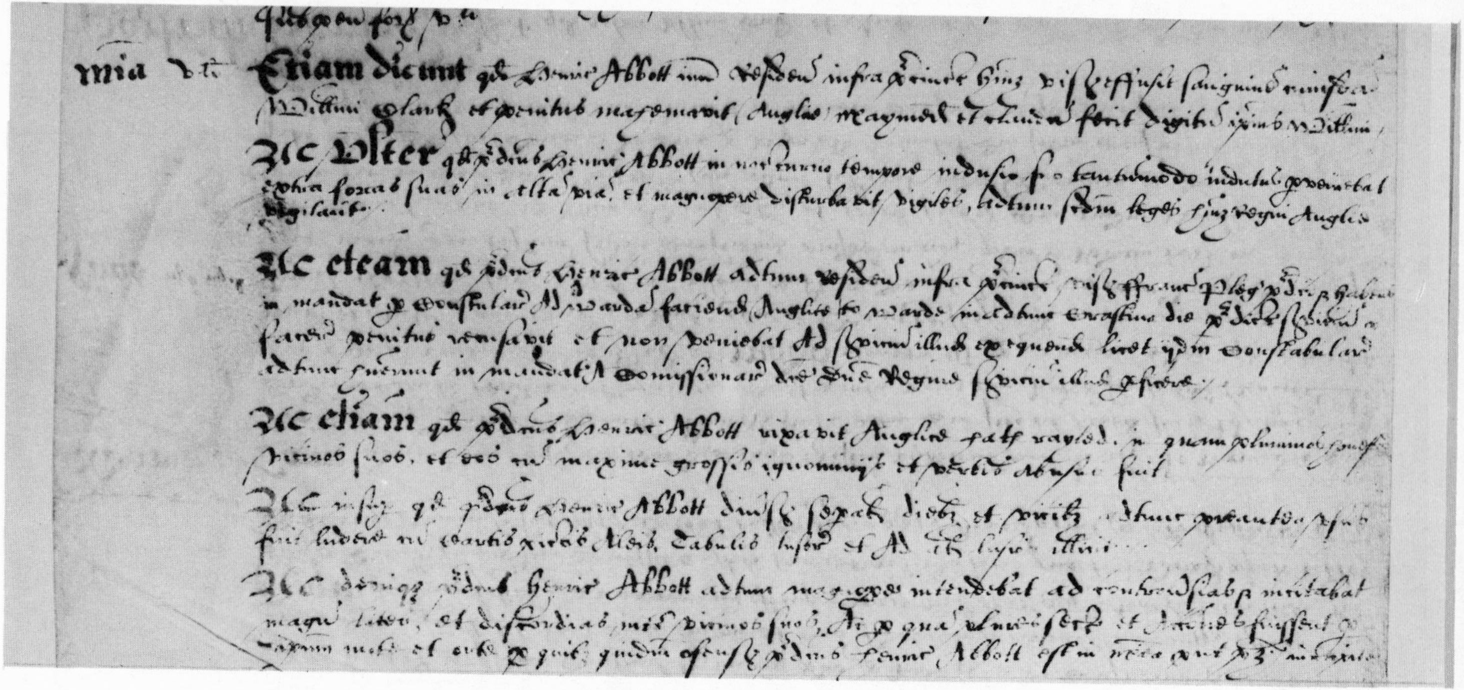

Figure 2:7 continued.

Ammercement vli Also they said that Henry Abbott junior resident within the precincts of this leet drew blood of one William Clark and utterly maimed and lamed the finger of the said William

And further that the foresaid Henry Abbott in the night time having on only his shirt came out of his doors into the high way and greatly disturbed the watchmen being then set in watch according to the laws of this realm of England

And also that the said Henry Abbott being then resident within the precincts of this leet and having charge of the Constables to ward next day did utterly refuse to do the said service and came not to perform the said service although the same Constables had commandment from the Commissioners of our soveregn Lady the Queen to do the same service

And also that the said Henry Abbott hath called upon many of his honest neighbours and abused them with very gross reproaches and words

And further that the said Henry Abbott at many days & times now past has played at cards & dice tables & other unlawful games

And finally that the said Henry Abbott was much given to contention and did stir up many strifes and discords between his neighbours whereby many suits actions were moved by him and grown for which offences the said Henry Abbott is ammerced as appears on his head

know a good deal concerning the administrative procedure
(Marchant 1969; Owen 1970; Stephens 1973: ch. 8). One
example of a presentment relating to a villager from Earls
Colne will indicate something of their nature: see figure
2:8. A combination of abbreviated latin, a fairly intricate
process and the sheer bulk of the documents, has meant that
much less use has been made of this source than one might
otherwise have expected.

The case illustrated above is not unrepresentative in
the amount of detail it gives or in its format. It is
difficult to generalize for the quality and survival of
ecclesiastical records varies enormously both temporally and
from jurisdiction to jurisdiction in England. The records
for the courts which covered the parish of Earls Colne are
excellent, particularly during the period 1570-1640. During
those years an average of about 20 cases a year were brought
to the various ecclesiastical courts relating to inhabitants
of Earls Colne. Each 'case' normally led to several
appearances as the trial proceeded. For the whole of this
seventy year period we are dealing with between 1,200 and
1,400 'cases', or something over three thousand separate
records if we treat each appearance as one instance. For the
short period when they exist in quantity, these documents
are the most intimate record of everyday life and tensions
that we possess. If we bear in mind that Earls Colne only
constituted a little over 1% of the population of one
county, it will be clear that the problem of analysing this
source on a regional basis are very great.

2:12 *Quarter Sessions.*
One jurisdiction which overlapped with that of the
court leet and ecclesiastical courts was that of the

Figure 2:8. An ecclesiastical court presentment.

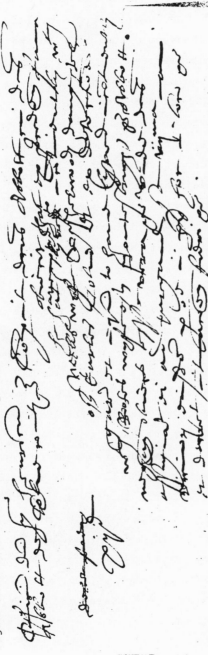

Office of the Judge against Henry
Abbott of Earles Colne

owes fees (crossed out)
xiid.

the said Abbott appeared against whom the
judge objected that on the basis of rumour
'he was accounted to have lyved incontinently with
Neels wyfe Ussherwoods daughter of Earles Colne'
and from the detection of the churchwardens 'to have
lyved incontinently with Rootes wyfe of Pontesbright &c'
Abbott denied the allegation to be true whence the judge
ordered him to purge himself under the hands of seven neighbours
of that parish at the next (court) in this place &c and ordered an
intimation to be made

Justices of Peace at the Quarter Sessions. The documents concerning the business of the Justices contains information relating to many topics including petty theft, bastardy, maintenance of the poor, highways and bridges. Considerable work has been done on this class of records in the early modern period and their content and nature has been thoroughly described. The records have already been used to study topics such as theft, witchcraft, riot, treatment of the poor (Guide to Essex Record Office 1969: 1-49; Stephens 1973: 55). Since the business could consist of many different types and could be brought to court in a number of ways, it is difficult to select a representative record. One example of a Quarter Sessions presentment for Earls Colne will give some indication of one kind of business: see figure 2:9. The records again vary from county to county both in quality and in their survival. Those for the county of Essex commence very early, in 1556, but in many counties they are not available until a century later. For Essex they continue in large quantities until the middle of the nine-teenth century. Although they survive for a longer period than do the ecclesiastical court records, they are less dense for specific years. Thus for Earls Colne during the period 1560-1710 there are, on average, between one and two Earls Colne cases a year surviving in the Quarter Sessions. During this hundred and fifty years, approximately 250 separate 'records' in all survive relating to this one parish. If the period were extended to the middle of the nineteenth century, we would still be dealing with no more than 500 separate references. The depositions, that is statements of witnesses and of the accused, are often extremely detailed and complex. An example of this type of document, which occasionally occurs in ecclesiastical and

Figure 2:9. A Quarter Sessions presentment.

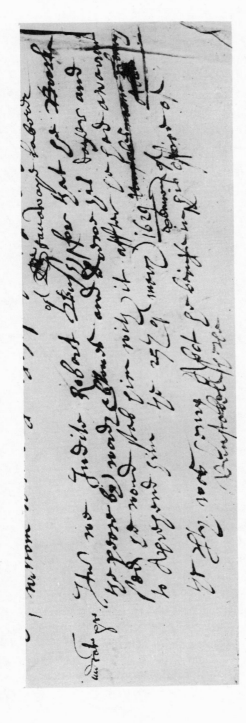

Item we Indite Robert Bush of Stanawaye laborer for that he Brack
the peece by words & bloues and drewe his dager and
sed he woud stab him with it afffter he had a warrent
to Aprehand him the 25th March 1629
the p(ar)ty was henry Abot he being in execution of his office of
Cunstabellshipe

Figure 2:10. An assize deposition.

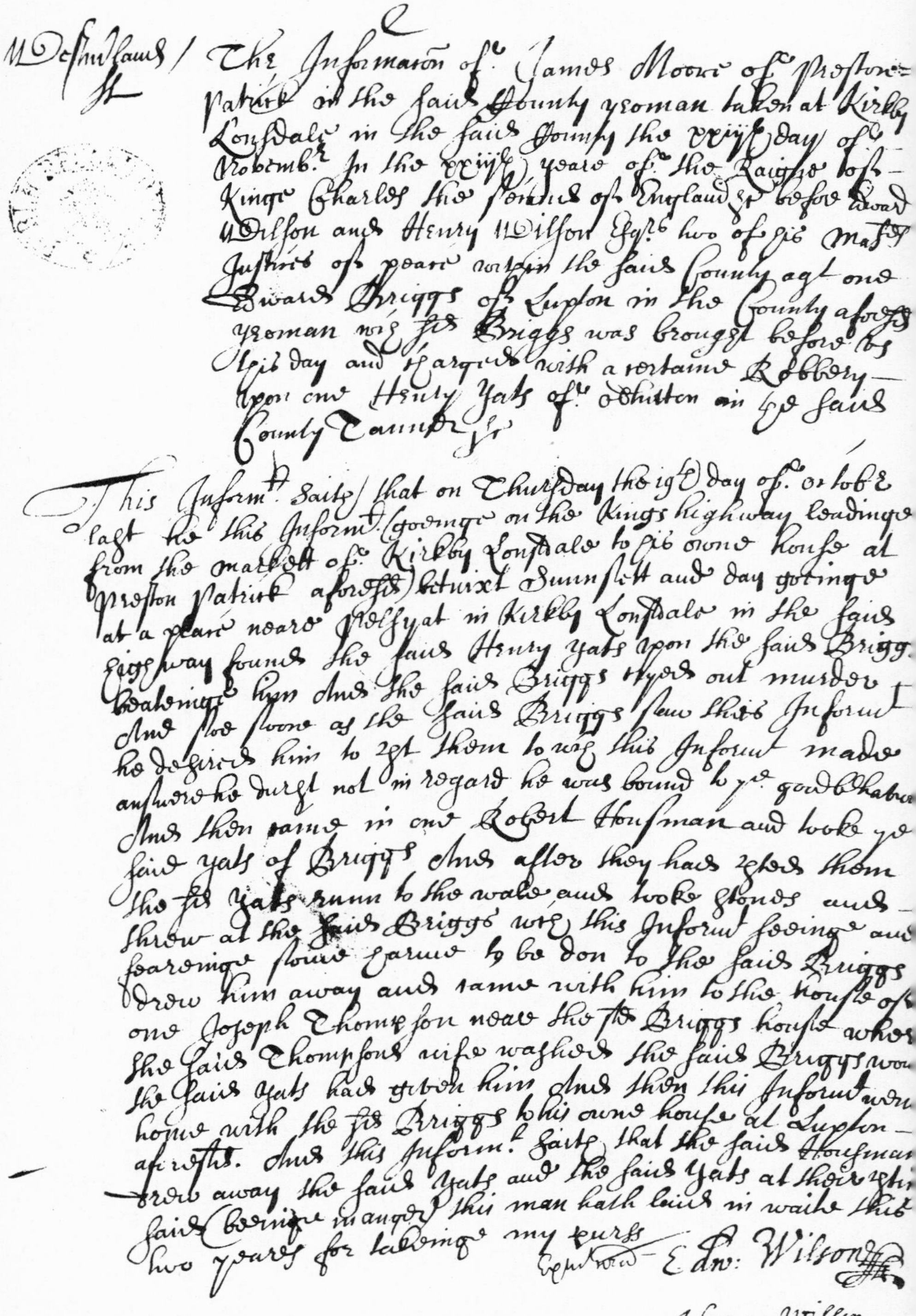

Figure 2:10 continued.

Westmorland The Informacion of James Moore of Preston
Patrick in the said County yeoman taken at Kirkby
Lonsdale in the said County the xxiiith day of
November In the xxxiiith yeare of the Raigne of
Kinge Charles the second of England &c before Edward
Wilson and Henry Wilson Esqrs two of his Majesties
Justices of peace within the said County agt one
Edward Briggs of Lupton in the County aforesd
yeoman wch sd Briggs was brought before us
this day and charged with a certaine Robbery
upon one Henry Yats of Oldhuton in the said
County Tanner &c

This Informant saith that on Thursday the 19th day of
October last he this Informant (goeinge on the Kings highway
leadinge from the Markett of Kirkby Lonsdale to his owne
house at Preston Patrick aforesaid) betwixt Sunnsett and
day goeinge at a place neare Pelsyat in Kirkby Lonsdale
in the said highway found the said Henry Yats upon the said
Briggs beateinge him And the said Briggs cryed out murder
And soe soone as the said Briggs saw this Informant he
desired him to part them to which this Informant made
answere he durst not in regard he was bound to the good
behaviour And then came in one Robert Housman and tooke the
said Yats of Briggs And after they had parted them the said
Yats runn to the wale and tooke Stones and threw at the
said Briggs which this Informant seeinge and feareinge some
harme to be don to the said Briggs drew him away and came
with him to the house of one Joseph Thompson neare the said
Briggs house where the said Thompsons wife washed the said
Briggs wound the said Yats had given him And then this
Informant went home with the said Briggs to his owne house
at Lupton aforesaid. And this Informant saith that the said
Housman drew away the said Yats and the said Yat at their
parting said (beeinge in anger) this man that laid in waite
this two yeares for takeinge my purse

> examined in the presence of
> Edward Wilson
> Henry Wilson

Quarter Sessions cases, may be examined under the next
court.

2:13 Assize.

As well as the local courts, whether of church or
county, there were numerous central courts, civil and
criminal, with jurisdiction over the villagers of Essex and
Cumbria. One of the most important of these were the Assize
courts. The records of these courts are now being extensively used by legal historians and there are a number of
good guides to both their quantity and the procedure which
produced the final documents (Cockburn 1972; Guide 1963).
One category of record within the general class may be
given, namely a deposition. This illustrates a general type
of document which is produced by most courts. The particular
deposition is one among a large set relating to coin
clipping, burglary and highway robbery in the Kirkby
Lonsdale region: see figure 2:10. Much more extensive
depositions than this are contained in the records of other
central courts such as Star Chamber and Chancery which have
not, as yet, been systematically used by investigators of
particular parishes.

2:14 Hearth Tax.

One of the classes of records most widely used by
historians is that created by the need for revenue on the
part of the State. Many studies have been made using
medieval and early modern taxation records, Lay Subsidies,
Hearth Tax and Land Taxes. The nature of these records is
now well known and there are numerous guides to their use
(Stephens 1973: 34). We may take as a representative of this
general class the seventeenth-century Hearth Taxes,

periodically levied during the reign of Charles II. Once
again these documents vary from county to county, both in
the degree to which they survive and in the way they were
assessed. An example of this type of record for Earls Colne
forms figure 2:11. In all, the document partially
illustrated below, lists 187 names. There are four other
surviving Hearth Taxes which cover Earls Colne during the
period 1660-75. Combined with the one above, they give us
a little over 700 names. Earlier tax documents for this
parish provide a total of about 600 names. By far the most
concentrated source are the Land Tax assessments, taken
yearly at the end of the eighteenth century and surviving
in Essex for most of the period 1780-1830. These record both
owner and occupier categories separately, even though the
people are fairly frequently the same, this source alone
produces over 10,000 names. The degree to which we can
estimate wealth structure in a parish, or the facts that we
can infer about named individuals from such records requires
much more investigation. Yet the records have many values
other than as a source for economic history. For example,
the Hearth Tax for some areas of England appear to have been
taken in house order, so that we can move along with the tax
assessor and reconstruct the size and location of houses.
Where occupiers are given, they provide a vital check on
manorial records, which frequently only give owners.

2:15 Will.

Last wills and testaments, in which individuals
bequeathed their movable property and sometimes immovable
also, were little used by historians until a few years ago.
Genealogists, however, were fully aware of their value.
There has been a rapidly growing interest in these records

Figure 2:11. A Hearth Tax.

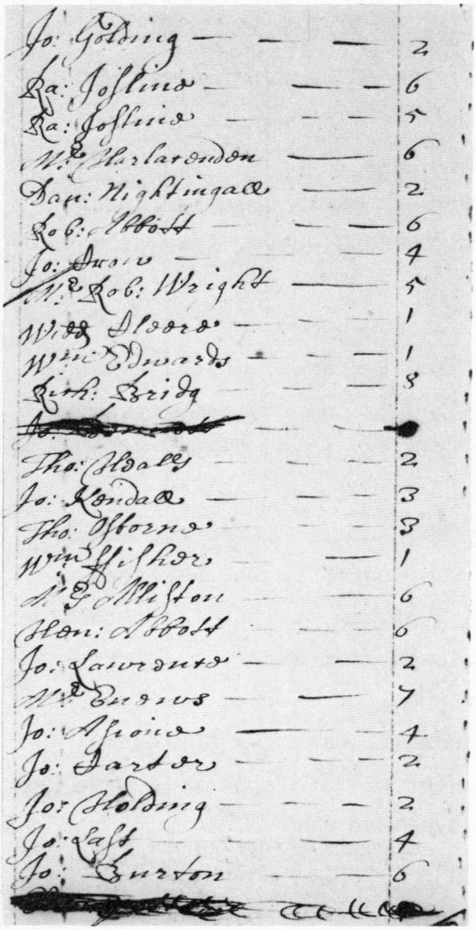

Jo: Golding	2
Ra: Josline	6
Ra: Josline	5
Mr Harlakenden	6
Dan: Nightingall	2
Rob: Abbott	6
Jo: Crow	4
Mr Rob: Wright	5
Widd Cleere	1
Wm: Edwards	1
Rich: Bridg	8
(Jo: Bennett, crossed out)	
Tho: Healls	2
Jo: Kendall	3
Tho: Osborne	3
Wm: Fisher	1
Mrs Alliston	6
Hen: Abbott	6
Jo: Lawrence	2
Mr Enews	7
Jo: Assione	4
Jo: Carter	2
Jo: Holding	2
Jo: Last	4
Jo: Burton	6
(one crossed through)	

and there is now an extensive literature on what they contain, where they are to be found and some of the difficulties in using them. Among the best general introductions are those of Camps and Spufford (Camps 1963; Spufford 1974: ch. 13). Though they varied considerably within a common form, wills were fairly standardized documents in the past. It is therefore not too difficult to give some idea of their content by citing one example from Earls Colne: see figure 2:12.

In some respects wills are the most complex and interesting of all local records since they combine information about property, religion, literacy, interpersonal relationships and a number of other topics. The number of wills and their quality is again very varied both in time and space. They appear to survive for most of England in considerable quantities from the early sixteenth century and continue in large numbers until the later eighteenth century. Some areas of England, for example some of the northern counties, have much higher ratios of wills to population than do others. Essex is not particularly favoured, yet the parish of Earls Colne has produced about 350 wills of persons residing in, or owning property in, the two manors during the period 1500-1800. On average, roughly 10 people are mentioned in each will, so that this constitutes references to over 3,000 persons. Only future analysis will establish who failed to make wills and in what ways the surviving wills are biased. What is certain is that this class of documents contains a very great deal of demographic, economic, social and other information which blends well with the other sources already described.

Figure 2:12. A will.

Figure 2:12 continued.

In the name of God Amen The Sixte day of November Anno Domine 1625 and in the First yeare of the Reigne of our Sovereigne Lord Charles by the grace of god of Greate Britaine Fraunce and Ireland Kinge Defender of the faith etc I Henry Abbot of Earles Colne in the Countie of Essex yeoman beinge in good and perfect remembrance thanks be given unto Almightie god therefoore I dooe make ordaine and Declare this my present last Will and Testament in mannour and foorme followinge First I commend my soule into the hands of Almightie god my creatour With an assured Faith and constant hope of eternall salvation and blessednesse amongst all the elect and Saints of god through the onely merits and passion of Jesus Christ my onely Saviour and Redeemer And my body to be buried in Christian sepulture in certaine hoope of the resurrection of the same unto everlasting life And for the dispoosinge of that portion of worldly goods wheerwith it hath pleased god in his greate love and favour to Indue me First I give and bequeath Unto Robert my sonne and to his heires and assignes forever all that my Customarie Tennement scittuated and being in Church streete in Earles Colne afooresaid with a garden plat and two crofts of land there unto belonging containing by estimation thre acres be it more or less with all and singuler their appurtenaunces as they are now in the tenure and occupation of Henry Abbot my sonne in Earles Colne afooresaid Provided alwaies and upon condition that my sonne Robert his heires or assignes shall pay or

Figure 2:12 continued.

cause to be paid unto Thomazin my beloved wife one Annuitie or yearely rent of Foure pounds of good and lawfull English money so longe as she shall remaine a widdow and no longer Item I give and bequeath unto Grace my daughter the somme of an hundred pounds of good and lawfull money of England to be paid unto her within six moneths next after my dissease Item I give and bequeath unto Francis Wright my brother in lawe five shillings of lawfull English money and to Grace my sister his wife tenne shillings of like lawfull money to be paid unto them within one moneth next after my dissease All the residue of my movable goods and Chattels debts bonds bills and specialties sommes of money and other personall rights whatsoever and howsoever due or owing unto me not given and bequeathed in and by this my present last will and Testament my debts that I owe beinge paid and my Funeralls discharged I wholly give unto Tomazin my beloved wife and to my two sonnes Henry and Robert whome I make and ordaine my true and lawfull executoures to see this my present last will and Testament truely and faithfully performed according to my true meaning and my trust reposed in them In witnesse whereof I dooe heerby utterly renounce and revoke all former wills made and declared by me whatsoever and have here unto put to my hand and seale the day and yeare first above written in the presents of theese witnesses

Robert Crow (signature of)   Henry Abbatt (signature of)

Daniel Lea (signature of)

William Adams Junior (signature of)

2:16 Probate inventory.

The other major probate records, which are often filed
with wills, are inventories of possessions. By
ecclesiastical law the administrators of estates were
required to present an inventory of the movable possessions
belonging to a man at his death. These goods were listed and
valued by neighbours and the inventory was shown at the
ecclesiastical court. This type of record has been widely
used, especially by historians of agriculture, and their
content and format is well known (Hoskins 1954: ch. 8;
Stephens 1973: 36-7, 111). The survival of these inventories
varies from county to county. Unfortunately most of the
inventories for the county of Essex have disappeared, except
for small areas or a few selected individuals. Very large
numbers of inventories have survived for the Archdeaconry
of Richmond, within which our sample parish of Kirkby
Lonsdale was situated. Consequently there are over 2,000
such inventories for Kirkby over the period 1550-1750. Each
inventory averages between 20 and 30 items of property, so
that one is dealing with about 50,000 items in all. On
average, each inventory contains between 10 and 15 names,
including that of the deceased and 4 witnesses. There are
therefore between 20,000 and 30,000 names in all. One
example of this source may be given: see figure 2:13.

A great deal of work needs to be done in order to
establish what exactly was omitted in inventories, how
accurate the valuations were, the bias in inventory making,
the degree to which the values changed with the point in the
life cycle at which they were made. There can be little
doubt as to the historical value of this class, however.
They not only provide information about the physical
setting, that is the housing, furniture, agriculture, nutri-

Figure 2:13. A probate inventory.

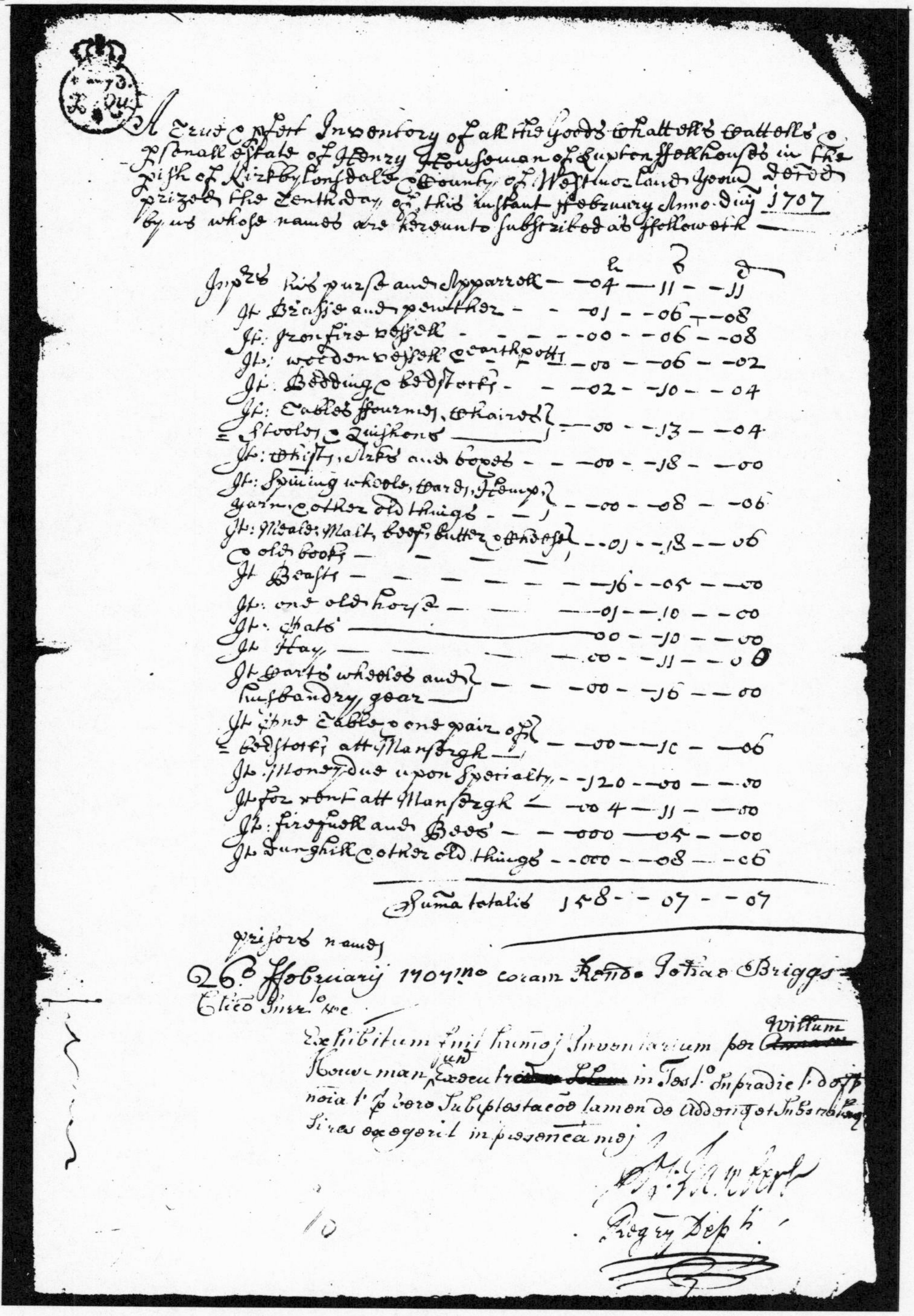

Figure 2:13 continued.

A true and perfect Inventory of all the Goods Chattells &
personal estate of Henry Houseman of Lupton Fellhouses in
the parish of Kirkby Lonsdale & County of Westmorland yeoman
deceased prized the Tenth day of this instant February Anno
domini 1707 by us whose names are hereunto subscribed as
followeth -

	li	s	d
imprimis his purse and Apparrell	4	11	11
Item Brasse and pewther	1	6	8
Item Iron fire vessell		6	8
Item wooden vessell & earth potts		6	2
Item Bedding & bedstocks	2	10	4
Item Tables Fourmes, Chaires Stooles & Quishons		13	4
Item Chists, Arks and boxes		18	0
Item Spinning wheele, Card, Hemp yarn & other old things		8	6
Item meale, Malt, beef, butter & Cheese, & old books	1	18	6
Item Beasts	16	5	0
Item one old horse	1	10	0
Item Oats		10	0
Item Hay		11	0
Item Carts wheeles and husbandry gear		16	0
Item One Table & one pair of bedstocks att Mansergh		10	6
Item Money due upon Specialty	120	0	0
Item for rent att Mansergh	4	11	0
Item firefuell and Bees		5	0
Item dunghill & other old things		8	6
Summa totalis	158	7	7

Prizors names (missing)

Proved 26th February 1707

tion, prices, but also material and social relationships.
The lists of debtors and creditors often appended to
inventories are invaluable as an index of interpersonal
relationships. Where inventories have survived, however,
their volume is once again an obstacle to their proper
exploitation.

2:17 Listing.

Formal censuses which list the inhabitants of England
exist at ten-year intervals from 1841. Before 1841 there are
a considerable number of listings for specific towns and
villages, taken for many different purposes. These early
listings have been used and described in a number of works
(Laslett in Wrigley 1966: ch. 5; Laslett 1972 : ch. 4;
Styles 1951-2). Where such early listings exist, they
provide unique information concerning who was actually
present at a point in time. One example can be given, for
the chapelry of Lupton within Kirkby Lonsdale in 1695. The
list was made to provide the basis for a new tax on
baptisms, marriages and burials, and batchelors over the age
of twenty-five: see figure 2:14. This particular listing was
taken for all the nine chapelries of Kirkby Lonsdale, and
covers the whole population of over 2,000 persons. Some of
the other chapelry listings are more detailed, giving name
and sex of children, for instance.

2:18 Summary and conclusion.

Anyone who is familiar with historical documents for
England will be aware that only a very small proportion of
the available records have been selected from the past. Yet
even these will show that there is a varied and rich set of
material, differing from parish to parish but often

Figure 2:14. A listing.

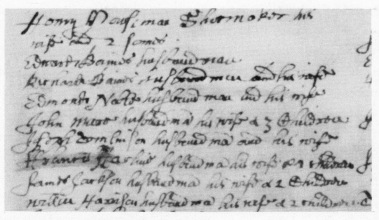

Henry Houseman Shoemaker his
wife and 2 sonnes

Edward Baines husbandman

Richard Baines husbandman and his wife

Edmond Noble husbandman and his wife

John Moore husbandman his wife & 3 Children

Joseph Tomlinson husbandman and his wife

Francis Harline husbandman his wife & 2 children

James Jackson husbandman his wife & 2 children

William Harrison husbandman his wife & 2 children

extending back for four or five hundred years. The sheer
size of the data in a well-recorded parish is somewhat over-
awing. If we guess that the twelve types of records
described above represent roughly two thirds of all the
material for an 'average' parish, we may make some general
estimates of the total amount of data for an area which
averaged about 1,200 persons over a period of some four
hundred years, between 1450 and 1850. All the records would
produce references to about 200,000 separate names to be
linked into specific individuals. Between one-sixth and one-
seventh of these names would come from the registers of
baptisms, marriages and burials. Total reconstitution from
all sources would, even at this level, take much longer than
'family reconstitution' based on one source. There would
also be the added labour of dealing with houses and land.
The records contain between 20,000 and 30,000 descriptions
of immovable property, similar to those indicated in the
manorial rental and transfer illustrated above. To index and
link these is a very considerable task. The major source for
movable items of property, the probate inventories, are
missing for the sample Essex village. A study of the Cumbria
parish of Kirkby Lonsdale, to which we have previously
alluded, would need to deal with between 40,000 and 60,000
items of property mentioned in this source. Finally, there
is the class of presentments for offences in the various
courts. The most numerous of these, as we have seen, were
the cases in the ecclesiastical courts and courts leet.
Between 6,000 and 8,000 such 'cases' probably survive for
Earls Colne over the whole period in all types of court. See
figure 2:15 for a detailed breakdown of these figures.

The sheer size of the documentation explains why many
of those who have attempted to undertake a 'total' study

Figure 2:15. Numbers of records for Earls Colne.

Class	Date covered	Number of names	land refs.	cases
Parish Register	1558-1858	30,000		
Rentals	1380-1880	30,000	12,000	
Court baron	1400-1900	30,000	7,000	
Frankpledge	1400-1750	25,000		
Court leet	1400-1750	10,000		
Church courts	1560-1750	5,000		3,000
Quarter sessions	1560-1750	1,000		250
Chancery	1550-1700	1,000		50
Hearth tax	1660-1700	1,000		
Wills	1500-1900	4,000		500
Inventories	1500-1750	(lost for Essex)		
C19 census	1841-1871			

notes:

1 The rounded figures and the fact that some of the columns are blank when it is obvious that they should not be indicate that these totals are based on projections from our present work and also on guesswork, rather than upon exact figures.

2 Movable items of property have been omitted. For example the roughly two thousand probate inventories for Kirkby Lonsdale contain about 25,000 names and describe approximately 50,000 items of property.

3 In order to make the table reflect a single real parish, rather than the best records for two, the twelve classes of documents are taken from the parish of Earls Colne alone. They are therefore not exactly the same as the twelve sample documents illustrated and discussed in the text.

4 In the case of church courts, each appearance in court is counted as one 'case'. The Quarter Sessions 'cases' include licensing and depositions.

have failed. It explains the great collections of notebooks
in which antiquarians painfully tried to transcribe the
records for particular communities. Their energies were
usually drained by the process, and they had little time to
reorder or analyse their findings.

Whereas an anthropologist deals with 1,000 or so
persons over one or two years, the investigator who tries
to chart a parish's history through time may be dealing with
very much larger numbers of persons. The task clearly
requires a new methodology. The following chapters are an
attempt to lay down some general guidelines. The problem is
a fairly obvious one. Given the kind of data which has been
presented in this chapter, how are we to analyse the documents so that they can be most efficiently integrated and
linked? For those who feel that it is not only an obvious
but also an easily soluble problem, the best plan would be
to stop at the end of this chapter and to sit down with a
pencil to see whether they could devise a way of doing it.
They will probably find, as we have done, that the task is
by no means trivial. Other readers may still not be
convinced that the data is of the quality to make it worth
even attempting such an analysis. Chapters 4 and 6 will
outline some features of the data, what it contains, its
shortcomings, and its value when compared to the material
collected by contemporary sociologists and social anthropologists. Chapter 5 provides a very brief survey of some of
the questions which may be asked of such data once it has
been indexed.

Chapter 3

MANUAL ANALYSIS OF THE DATA

3:1 Introduction.

Marc Bloch wrote that 'one of the most difficult tasks
of the historian is that of assembling those documents which
he considers necessary' (1954: 69). We must include under
'assemble' not only the gathering of records into one place,
but the further indexing and analysing of these records in
such a way that they may more easily be used. Both these
processes may appear to the non-historian to be fairly
trivial matters, yet upon the methods of collecting and
preparing the data for subsequent analysis will depend the
whole success or failure of a project concerned with
studying a particular community. As Bloch further remarked,
'to neglect to organize rationally what comes to us as raw
material is in the long run only to deny time – hence,
history itself' (1954: 147). Two things are absolutely
essential. The first is that one has available as full,
complete and exact a copy of all the records relating to the
population being studied as possible. Without this, as
stressed in the previous chapter, any attempt at a 'total'
study is doomed. Secondly, once obtained, the material must
be broken down in various ways by means of indexing so that
it becomes practicable to ask complex questions. The records
as they exist in the archives were not organized to help the
social investigator.

This chapter will consider some strategies which we have adopted to collect together then break down the types of record described in the previous chapter by hand. A later volume will describe methods for breaking down the same records using a computer. The two methods are complementary.

The necessity to obtain complete transcripts of all relevant documents cannot be stressed too greatly. Whenever abstracts are made, it later appears that one has omitted something of importance. Even full transcripts are not really satisfactory for it is frequently necessary to return to the original handwriting in order to check ambiguities. This need for an exact copy would seem to pose an insuperable problem for, as we have seen, the records for any one parish are often immense. To transcribe them in full at the archives, as our Victorian forebears found, could occupy many months or years and even then one would only have an unsatisfactory copy, rather than the original.

Even if it were possible to overcome the transcription difficulty it would seem to be extremely difficult to devise an uniform and satisfactory way of rearranging the material so that it could be used more economically and swiftly. The basic principle of the indexing required to make access to the records possible is that each index must, in essence, be devoted to a major theme, for example, name, place, subject. Within each index the separate records, or 'cards' in a card index, relate the major theme to one other piece of information. However much is written on a specific card or sheet, when one is looking at it at a particular moment, one is looking for a single connection between two pieces of information, for example, between a name and a place or a date and an event. A good deal of research consists of breaking down material into its supposed 'constituent ele-

ments', and then building it up again, thus correlating
areas which have previously been artificially held apart by
the original ordering of the information. This principle of
'one fact on one card', 'fact' being defined as an
interrelation between two pieces of information, is of crucial importance in many branches of research, and is widely
recognized.

Efficient indexing is the essential research tool for
any really fruitful study of the kind envisaged here. The
success or failure of historical reconstruction will largely
depend on the sophistication and thoroughness of the
indexing. When attempting to solve problems, it is
absolutely essential that one should be able to move very
quickly along a series of links, a chain of names or events
or places, in order to see whether some hypothesis is
correct. If such movement is very arduous or time-consuming,
the tenuous thread will be lost. The social anthropologist
or sociologist can operate by using the flexibility and
linking capacity of the human brain, using the memory and
synthesizing power of both himself and his informants. By
asking the right questions in the right order he can elicit
complex information. The final aim of an investigator of
past communities attempting to study similar problems is to
build his information around him in such a form that he can
approach as closely as possible to the social scientist's
privileged position, but in relation to a far larger body
of data than that usually available to any specific social
investigator. The following is a description of one attempt
to come to grips with very large bodies of material using
manual-indexing methods.

3:2 Location and transfer of records.

In England, the stage of locating and copying the original documents relating to a specific area in the past has been transformed by two major developments which have occurred since 1960. Before that date it would have been impossible to have attempted the kind of project described in this book. The records for particular places were scattered and unindexed, their whereabouts were often unknown. Even when located, they were often found to be in private hands or in large repositories where they could not be found amidst the piles of other documents. Since the last war, and with increasing momentum, there has been an archival revolution. The two main features of this change have been the widespread establishment of local Record Offices in most counties and large towns, and a vastly improved systems of listing and indexing the records which were deposited in them. The result has been that many records which were previously in private hands have now become accessible and others which could not be found have now been listed. It is very hard in the later 1970s to envisage the difficulties facing the historian of local communities before about 1960. It would certainly have been impossible to have attempted, for example, the study of Kirkby Lonsdale in Cumbria for the records, including the important listing of the parish in 1695 and the voluminous manorial records at Lowther Castle, were either undiscovered or unavailable. For the first time since the parishes actually existed in the past, their records have become visible and adequate guides and indexes have appeared.

Even when the records have become visible they could still elude us since their bulk would make it impossible to copy them out as a preliminary to analysis. For example,

during the last century a number of local historians were
interested in the parish of Kirkby Lonsdale and spent many
months transcribing the records, including the wills at
London, manor court books in private hands, and the parish
registers. Yet their combined years of labour have merely
produced a very partial selection from the voluminous
records. Furthermore, the local historians who transcribed
records lived in a more leisurely age, supported on clerical
or other stipends which allowed them to spend many months
browsing and copying the documents. The modern student often
has less time and simply cannot afford to go to London or
Preston for a year at a time while he transcribes every
single word. Even if he could do so, he would be well aware
that even his most careful efforts at accurate transcripts
will contain errors. Fortunately, during the same period as
the material became available, there was a photographic
revolution. The development of various techniques of
photocopying documents, including xeroxing, microfilming and
microfiche, has helped the student of past communities.
Again this may seem to non-historians to be a technological
change of no great importance. Until one has faced 2,000
probate inventories for one parish, or hundreds of feet of
manor court roll, it is difficult to see how the development
of photography can alter the very nature of the questions
we ask. Yet it seems likely that the use of photocopies of
original documents in the study will come to be recognized
as a step of the same magnitude as the break with tradition
in social anthropology whereby, in the early part of this
century, Malinowski started to work in the original language
of the society he was studying, rather than through an
interpreter. It has freed the historian so that he can
undertake a depth of analysis hitherto barred by the sheer

practical impossibility of bringing together all the
original material into one place.

Merely locating the material for a specific place in
the past can be a fairly lengthy process since records tend
to be very widely scattered in England. Many of the documents will be stored in the local Record Office and the
first step is to enquire there. But a very large quantity
will still be in private hands, in central repositories in
London, and elsewhere. For example, the ecclesiastical court
records relating to Kirkby Lonsdale are distributed between
Carlisle, Chester, Leeds, London, Preston and York. Even
when the place of deposit is discovered, it may take a
considerable time to find the records relating to a
particular parish, especially if one is searching through
the records of a court which covers the whole of England.
It is for this reason, among others, that the records of
such central courts as Chancery, King's Bench and Star
Chamber have remained practically unused by local
historians. Yet there are now a growing number of very good
guides to the nature and location of records (Guide to Essex
Record Office 1969; Guide to Public Records 1963; Hoskins
1959; Stephens 1973). The availability of such guides makes
it unnecessary to expand on the problems of locating documents.

The final aim is to transfer all the material from its
scattered resting places to one's study so that it can be
thoroughly investigated. The method for doing this will vary
with each document and each research worker, but some
general remarks as to how we have proceeded may be of
interest to others since there has been little discussion
in print concerning the effects of the recent advances in
photography on historical research.

There are two major choices open to a research worker who is faced with a document or pile of documents which he wishes to 'transfer' from one place to another. The first is the degree to which the document will be altered even as it is first transcribed. Is it to be shortened by just taking abstracts, or is it to be reordered with a view to future analysis, or is it to be translated if it is in a foreign language? For example, when faced with a large number of cases in a particular court which all have a common form, it may be thought sensible to copy out the cases in a standard and reordered format, taking several spare carbon copies at the same time. The document can then, without further time-consuming copying and reordering, be broken down under a number of headings. An example of this in relation to ecclesiastical court records will be given below. Yet there are serious drawbacks to such a reordering which will also be discussed later.

The second major decision concerns the technical medium or method of copying. If one has decided to obtain an unchanged transcript it will save enormous periods of time and labour if a photocopy can be made. Also all manual transcripts need to be double-checked since errors in transcription are bound to occur. Furthermore, the exact location of words on the page, the style of the handwriting, the pieces which are crossed out, all these often turn out to be important at a later date and can only be partially and with great difficulty captured in a handwritten or typed transcript. Microfilms are far cheaper than xerox copies and are easier to store. Certain documents, such as court rolls, are often too bulky to be photographed in any other way. Furthermore, if one uses an ordinary 35mm slide projector, cuts up the microfilm and mounts it as slides, it is possible to enlarge the original document several times by projecting it onto a wall. When the original is difficult to decipher, it is often much easier to read in this form. On the other hand, microfilms are in some ways less easy to work with. It is difficult to type directly from them or to find a particular page on a roll of microfilm (although slides can be numbered and indexed), than on a sheet of xerox. One of the major considerations in deciding whether to photocopy the documents or transcribe them by hand at the archive, apart from money and the availability of photographic facilities, is the degree to which the information one needs is concentrated. Information concerning a particular place that is concentrated in blocks, such as a parish register or manor court roll, is ideal for photographic treatment. Records that lie scattered and embedded in other documents of less relevance, for instance the material in ecclesiastical and secular courts, may be very wasteful to photograph. A compromise which deals with some situations is to tape-record verbatim documents which are very long, yet are not of the right texture or sufficiently numerous to photograph, such as the long depositions in certain central courts. This last option, as well as the possibility of using a typewriter, depends entirely on the facilities of the archive where the research is being conducted. It may also be worth learning shorthand in order to save time at the Record Office.

When one has made a copy of the original document so that it can be worked on at one's own convenience the real work of analysis has still not begun. Yet such copying has absorbed a large proportion of the total energy of a great band of local historians. If it is decided to take a short cut and to save time by restructuring the records as they are copied at the archive, it is essential that one not only understands the documents completely at this early stage, but also that one has a clear idea of the kind of questions one is likely to ask. This is necessary not only so that the reordered transcripts are sensibly arranged, but also because it is very likely that implictly or explicitly a decision will be taken to omit certain, apparently redundant and irrelevant, information when making the reordered transcript. Later it is very likely that one will find that what was left out is vitally important: it is not always possible to go back and find it, or go back to unscramble one's apparently foolproof reordering to obtain what turns out to be the essential order of the original. Since, in practice, it appears that one cannot either fully understand the documents until they have all been assembled and one can compare them, nor can one specify in advance the full range of questions one will be interested in, the short-cut turns out to be a long way round. The course of wisdom, if one is to be fully satisfied, is to keep reordering and omission at this stage to an absolute minimum.

3:3 Indexing the data by hand.

The major stages in transcribing and indexing documents by hand are as follows:

1 Locate the document.
2 Make a copy for reference, preferably by photographic means.
3 Transcribe fully and translate into English if necessary, taking carbon copies for indexes.
4 Check the transcript against the copy or the original.
5 Abstract names for the personal name index.
6 Cut up carbon copies for indexes by place, subject etc.

7 Sort name, place and subject indexes.

8 Link cards to identify specific people, places etc.
The first four stages have been described in the previous
section. They may be done in the archive or at home; several
of the processes may be done in one operation, but it is
necessary to distinguish them for purposes of analysis. The
final product of these stages for us is an exact, English,
typewritten or handwritten, version of the original, with
several spare carbon copies, or xerox copies. One copy of
this will be filed by source. We use different coloured
springback files to denote the major sources, for example,
manorial - red, ecclesiastical - green, courts other than
ecclesiastical - blue. All these stages are necessary
whether one is going to index and process the documents by
hand or by computer.

The next four stages are peculiar to a hand-indexing
system and are extremely time consuming. For many types of
search the human mind and eye are more efficient than a
computer and the best way to solve a problem is to use a
hand index. The following account of producing such an index
by hand is based on practical experience with Essex and
Cumbrian parishes during the years 1963-77. There are five
principal ways of classifying the information by hand; by
source, name, subject, date, place. It is necessary to be
able to move both within an index and between indexes, for
example from name to name, date to date, name to date to
subject to place and so on. This can be represented simply
as in figure 3:1. The creation of all the possible types of
index under these five headings, for example name by date,
name by place, name by subject etc., would mean that the
information would have to be arranged in 25 different
indexes or five times five. At present we have found that

the following general indexes are the most useful, though
others will no doubt emerge:

1   Source index:

Complete transcripts of each source, arranged by date
within source and kept in coloured files.

2   Personal name index:

Cross-references to every personal name, on small
coloured cards organised alphabetically.

3   Separate name indexes to specific sources:

At present we have these for: Hearth Tax, will-makers,
parish registers of neighbouring parishes, Josselin's
diary and the Harlakenden Account Book.

4   General place index:

All references to particular houses or plots of land:
alphabetical by name of place.

5   Manorial transfers, to:

All transfers of property in the court rolls, organized
alphabetically under the names of the persons who
recieved the property.

6   Manorial transfers, from:

As above, but organised by the names of the people from
whom the property was transfered.

7   Rental Index:

Figure 3:1. Major types of index.

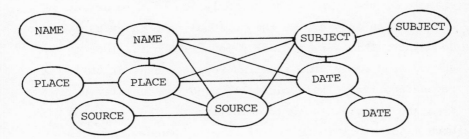

All rentals and surveys, organised alphabetically by
the names of the holders of the land.

8 Map index:

Abstracts of records, showing for each field or house
the names of all owners and residents, from a sixteenth-century map to the Tithe Award map. All sources
are incorporated; the index is linked to a numbered map
and organised under property number.

9 General subject index:

Full transcripts of cases from various courts,
including the court leet, Quarter Sessions,
ecclesiastical courts, and also from other sources such
as wills, diaries etc. Organised under topics such as
'godchildren', 'murder', bastardy', 'weather' etc.

10 Court index:

Full transcripts of appearences in all courts, from
court leet to Star Chamber, organised alphabetically by
person; includes ownership of freehold land, common
recoveries etc. as well as criminal offences.

It will be seen that about one dozen major indexes, or about
half of the possible types, have been created. This allows
swift access to the records in a number of different ways.

The indexes listed above can be broken down into two
major classes. Those produced by abstracting from a record,
and those where the whole of a record is included. The major
example of the former, and probably the most important of
all research indexes, is the personal name index to all
documents. This was originally modelled on the idea of
abstracting names from a parish register central to 'family
reconstitution'. It is basically used for identifying
separate individuals, or record linkage. The cards set links
both within this index and to other indexes. It has to be

an abstract, yet the abstract must be full enough to allow
the reconstitution of individuals from this index alone,
with pointers to all the sources of this information.
Through the matching of records within this one index all
the other indexes are invisibly drawn together into a
complex skein or web. The nature of the index can again best
be illustrated by a diagram, showing the various fields
which may occur on a name index card. These fields, or the
information in them, act as concentrated sets of pointers
between records. Each card must refer to only one 'event',
in other words one appearance of one person in one document
at one point in time. The information must not be expanded
too greatly. If they become stores of information, rather
than abstracts used for matching, this will destroy their
purpose, for they will merely become another replication of
the data in its entirety and too large to handle. Yet each
one needs to contain not only an accurate reference to its
origin, but also information which will fall into any of the
following criteria for matching two cards against each other
in order to determine whether they refer to the same person:
surname, forename, father's forename, mother's forename,
date of birth, date of death, marital status, spouse's name,
date of marriage. Figure 3:2 shows how these information
fields may be arranged on an index card.

The card is filed under the name and all the information on it is related to that individual, for example, he
is a butcher and constable. The card thus points one into
the other indexes of place, subject and source, as well as
to the name index under Henry's father, William. Most cards,
of course, do not contain most of these fields; examples
derived from particular sources will be given in the
following sections. A further practical constraint is size;

Figure 3:2. Model of a name index card, with an example of a complete card (hypothetical).

```
FORENAME SURNAME
        OCCUPATION
              PLACE

RELATION TO OTHER NAME

OTHER NAME

ROLE IN EVENT

EVENT

OFFICE

SOURCE

                DATE

ARCHIVAL REFERENCE
```

```
Henry ABBOTT    butcher
            of Masons tenement

        son of

William ABBOTT

accused of

theft

Constable

Quarter Sessions

                1/12/1635

QSR 290/29
```

in our system cards are cut to two and a half inches by
three inches, half a standard five by three card. If they
are any bigger the resulting indexes would be colossal. Even
on very thin paper and on these small cards, a name index
for a parish of 1,200 persons for a period of 400 years is
likely to occupy many cubic feet of space, or several dozen
filing cabinet drawers.

All the other main indexes take the whole of a record,
for example with a land transfer or court case we use a
standard size index card five inches by three inches, and
fold long items to conform to the standard card. Since each
index uses a different key under which the document will be
arranged, it is essential for the sake of speed of searching
to have some way of drawing the human eye to the central
key. Originally a system of reordering the document, for
example so that personal names came near the top of a card,
sources at the bottom, was devised. This has several
advantages when searching, for information concerning
different fields can be found quickly and a certain amount
of abbreviation and coding can also be undertaken at the
same time. In practice, a number of our hand indexes are
constructed in this way and they will be illustrated in the
following sections. On the basis of experience, however, we
have finally come to the conclusion that the saving in time
when searching does not justify such a restructuring for
there are two serious defects which arise from this method.
Firstly, it takes much longer to type a copy from the
original document since the original word order is not used
and the eye has to search ahead for information from the
later part of the record which may need to be put near the
start of the restructured version. With the very great
number of records to be processed, this is a serious matter.

Secondly, it leads to various kinds of inaccuracy. Not only does the greater effort needed to resort the information lead to mistakes, but, as suggested above, a stage of abbreviation and coding is slipped in here. In order to compress and save time, phrases are turned into single words and different but apparently similar words are standardized. If this were were done absolutely consistently the harm would not be great. But not only is it impossible for several different workers, working over months and years, to be consistent, but it is impossible to recover from mistaken coding. It is thus becoming clear that while it may help to guide the eye in certain ways, for example by the use of capital letters or underlining, the text should be transcribed in full and in the original order. Figure 3:3 shows the two systems. The original record consisted of a flow of words which appeared to contain the information fields 'A', 'B', 'C', 'D'. In example 1 the fields are located on different parts of the page and in example 2 the relevant field is indicated by underlining. It has been found that the documents themselves are almost always sufficiently structured so that, once one understands their form, it is possible to find information 'fields' quickly. The original order may turn out to be important later and

Figure 3:3. Two ways of indexing.

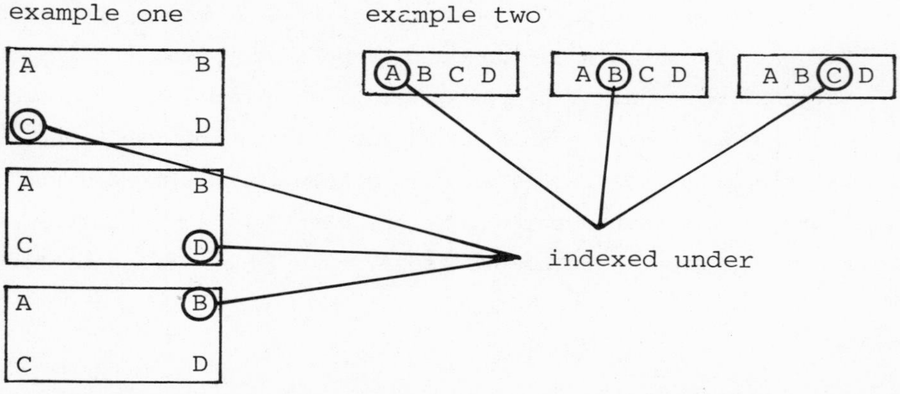

to destroy it just to help the searching is unsatisfactory.
It is better to mark or underline and not to interfere with
the original text.

Another point we have learnt from bitter experience is
that transcribing, indexing and linking together records
which refer to the same person are separate stages and must
not be conflated however much, in the short run, this
appears to save time and paper. Thus, for example, our
method of indexing the ecclesiastical court records,
illustrated below, where several presentments apparently
made against the same person were put together when
transcribing from the original document, is unsatisfactory
and leads to error. The general rule of only one event on
one card must be adhered to.

The various types of index which have already been
found to be of use and moderately easy to create by hand
have been outlined above. It will be seen that various kinds
of subject index are beginning to be made. It is likely that
the subject indexes will grow dramatically partly because
such indexes are not only indexes in themselves, but are,
in fact, substantive results in their own right. Other
indexes, for example an index of all occupations or statuses
mentioned, or of all the sources by date order, with every
event occurring on each successive day in the village
indicated, would be most useful.

The following sections are included for two purposes.
To document the system which we currently use and hence
provide a guide to those who wish to consult our indexes,
and to provide an historical account of how our hand-
indexing system emerged. It must be stressed, however, that
it should not be taken as a model. As repeatedly stated
above, we have now come to the conclusion that the best

method is to type the original record verbatim, in an English translation, and not to restructure it at all. As a model, therefore, we would suggest that the direct transcript of the original given in chapter 2 above, with suitable underlining or other marks to help the eye, would be the best form in which the document could be transcribed for the hand indexes.

3:4 Parish register.

There is little need to alter parish register entries except to abbreviate them to save space and time. Our re-structured version is shown in figure 3:4.

We type a top copy, which is kept in a file so that one can look up by the source, and three carbon copies are made. Each entry in the register is glued onto a yellow card. The colour coding may seem unimportant at first, but it makes information retrieval from the central name index much faster. We did not originally employ such a colour code in the Kirkby Lonsdale study and found that it took much longer to retrieve information. The use of glue, rather than staples which we originally used, is also essential. Staples turn out to be hopelessly unmanageable. It is perhaps worth mentioning that we have found that small quantities of wallpapering adhesive made up from powder is more efficient and economical than buying pots of glue.

Parish register entries often contain two or more names, for example, John son of Peter X was baptized. Such an entry needs to be filed under both John and under Peter. In such cases the person under whom the card is to be indexed needs to be underlined, as in the example below. The second carbon copy can be cut up and used for such double-name instances. When there are more than two names in an

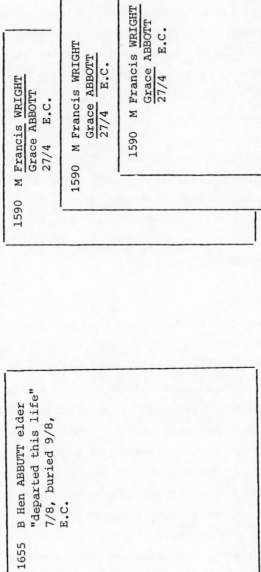

Figure 3:4. Example of a parish register card.   *Figure 3:5.* Cards generated by a marriage entry.

entry, the third carbon copy is used. Marriages are more
complicated since not only are there two partners, but two
cards need to be made for the woman, in order to record and
link her incarnations as a married and unmarried woman. An
example of the cards generated by a marriage appears as
figure 3:5. The principles of abstracting such small records
have already been widely discussed by those practising
family reconstitution. The method above is merely a slight
modification of their approach and draws heavily, for
example, on their methods of dealing with marriage links
(Wrigley 1966: 123).

With a parish register it is also necessary at some
point to start abstracting certain entries into the subject
index; there are references to bastards, deaths of
strangers, twins, suicides, epidemics and other matters.
Basically this is a very simple source which mainly creates
information for the general name index.

3:5 Manorial rental.

Manorial rentals, which deal with land and other
property as well as people, are more complicated documents
and our original restructured versions attempted to deal
with this fact by a more fundamental reordering of the
information. Our present version of a rental transcript card
is shown in figure 3:6. The small card in the same figure
is an example of the very much abbreviated abstracts used
in the main name index. These abstracts are made on blue
cards, to indicate that they come from manorial records.
This, and the other examples in this chapter, correspond to
the full transcripts in chapter 2

Rentals have an added dimension in that they tell us a
good deal about property ownership and they therefore need

Figure 3:6. Rental cards.

```
Hen ABBOTT sen & wife Joane              1638   E.C.   20/4

In reversion after the death or their mother
3 crofts called Husses.        Copy.    Rent 1/3
Reversion to
2a. in the Common Meade.       Copy.    Rent 2/-
Reversion to
croft called Sandehills 1r.    Copy.    Rent 1/-

            Hen ABBOTT sen

            copyhold called Husses
            & other property
```

Figure 3:7. Manor court transfer card.

```
Hen ABBOTT dec       C.P.  At a court held Tuesday 22
                     June 10 Eliz., H.A. was admitted
Hen ABBOTT           to one tenement with two crofts
  nephew/            of land containing 2a and
                     a garden adjoining situate in
12/1616              Church Street in Colne to hold
                     to him and his heirs for ever.
Now it is found that the aforesaid H.A. died before
this court thus seized and that H.A. his nephew is
the nearest heir.  H.A. admitted.
```

to be integrated into various place indexes. We have found
by experience that the two most important place indexes are
as follows. One is organized by the name of the property.
This enables one to look up all references to a named piece
of land or house. A second is organized by the name of the
owner.

3:6 *Manor court transfer.*

Manorial transfers can be dealt with in a similar way
to rentals, though they tend to be longer entries and more
complex. An added copy needs to be taken in order to deal
with the two owners mentioned. The example we have chosen
is a relatively short and simple one. The main transcript
card is ahown as figure 3:7. It will be seen that, as in the
rental, information on certain topics is located on certain
areas of the card. This fixed format approach makes it
easier to hunt through an index primarily organized, for
example, for names or dates. Typing surnames in capitals and
underlining would, however, be almost as efficient and the
extra labour and inaccuracies of the system, as mentioned
above, suggests that it would be better to type the document, with some abbreviations, exactly as in the original.

As with rentals, the top copy is kept exactly in the
order in which it appears in the original document. One
carbon copy is cut up and glued onto cards and sorted under
the name of the place. We have found it most useful to
create two indexes for land transfers, one for persons from
whom, the other for persons to whom, property is
transferred. Every name, whether of past owners, witnesses
to the transaction, those acting for the bailiff, or in any
other capacity, is abstracted onto blue cards and put into
the name index. These cards should not only carry the name

and date and source, but also the role of the individual in
the transfer, for example 'owner of tenement'. With an
estimated five thousand or more names in the manorial courts
for the parish of Earls Colne over the whole historical
period, it can be seen that this is no small task.

3:7 The view of frankpledge.

Although they constitute lengthy records, the lists of
names of those who owed suit of court in views of
frankpledge are simple documents, even simpler to deal with
than the parish register. An exact transcript of the document is made for our files and each name is abstracted onto
a blue card for the name index. The cards derived from the
last three names in the example form figure 3:8.

3:8 Court leet.

Figure 3:9 shows three of the cards which would be
abstracted from the sample court leet cases. Once again the
top copy would be kept with the rest of the source, that is
within the full transcript of the court rolls. All the names
would be abstracted onto small blue cards, one of which is
shown in the figure.

One problem that interests us is the overlap of courts.
Do people who appear in the court leet also appear in
Quarter Sessions? Does a particular case move from court to
court? For this reason we have an index, by the name of the
accused, of all court appearances. A problem which faces us
with all court records other than land transfers is that
whatever subject index headings we chose, they are likely
to be arbitrary and idiosyncratic. Yet it is obviously
better to bring together cases which seem to be concerned
with the same type of action, than not to attempt this at

Figure 3:8. Cards from a view of frankpledge.

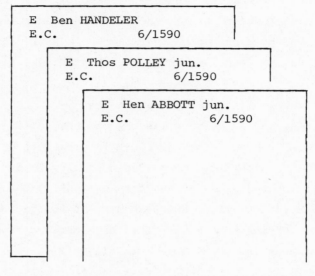

```
E   Ben HANDELER
E.C.            6/1590
        E   Thos POLLEY jun.
        E.C.            6/1590
                E   Hen ABBOTT jun.
                E.C.            6/1590
```

Figure 3:9. Cards from a court leet presentment.

```
Present Hen ABBOTT jun resident within the precincts
of this leet for drawing blood of Wm CLARK and
"utterlie maimed and lamed the finger of the said Wm"
amercement for this and other offences £5

    Present Hen ABBOTT jun that "in the night time havin
    on onely his shirte" came out of his doors in the hi
    way and greatly disturbed the watchmen "being then s
    in watche" according to the lawes of this Realme of
    England.
    amercement for this and other offences £5

            Hen ABBOTT jun

            assault on Wm CLARK

E.

        E.C.   Leet                          7/1592
```

all. For example, at present the court leet cases are
arranged under some of the following headings in our index:
aliens - harbouring strangers; assault; drink - drunken
behaviour, enclosure - unlawful enclosure; licence - to keep
an alehouse or practice as a baker or butcher; office -
offences relating to official duties.

It will be obvious that someone who was primarily
interested, for example, in bakers and brewers, might have
an index which cut across the ones listed above to pick up
all references to baking and brewing. The divisions have
been designed to be general enough to be able to deal with
material not only from the court leet, but also from other
contemporary courts. Only thus will it be possible to see
how various actions overlapped and moved between the courts.
The distinctions also tend to be based, as much as possible,
on the offences as they were seen by officials at the time,
rather than on our own distinctions. We have found that it
is surprisingly easy to index almost all of the court
material without hesitation or the need to index the same
offence two or three times under separate headings within
a fairly narrow range of topics, not more than forty in all.

3:9 *The ecclesiastical court.*

Ecclesiastical court records are somewhat more complex
than the court leet cases, but basically they can be dealt
with in the same way. The main problem is that whereas the
court leet cases are specific to manors within the parish,
the ecclesiastical cases come from the Archdeaconry Act
books which cover the whole deanery of Lexden and references
to Earls Colne are sporadic. Thus it is expensive to
microfilm them. The format described below was devised after
considerable experimentation and allows one to start

indexing even while working on the original records in a Record Office. It is therefore efficient in terms of time, space, and ease of searching. It suffers from the drawbacks mentioned above in that it may easily distort the original record and lead to coding and oversimplification. If one were starting again, therefore, it would be best to take exact transcripts of the original. This system is described here partly as an historical record, partly as a guide to our less than perfect, but already existing, system. As these records take a long time to search, the following form was devised to speed up the process of transcription and also to make it unnecessary to reindex the records once they had been transcribed. The form was also devised to take into account the special ecclesiastical process and jargon. The card generated by the sample case is shown as figure 3:10. We use green cards in the name index for all appearances in the ecclesiastical court. For the subject index, we face the

Figure 3:10. Ecclesiastical court card.

Hen ABBOTT of E.C.

app. objected "that he is
accounted to have lived
incontinently with Neells
wife Ussherwoods daughter
of E.C." and detected by
wardens "to have lyved
incontinently with Rootes
wife of Pontisbright";
denies- to P/7 and
intimation to be made.

8/258   8/1/1579/80

same problems of classification that were found with the
court leet. Some of the headings within which it has been
found possible to place the ecclesiastical court cases
without doing them too much violence are as follows:
administration – of wills; attendance – at church; doctrine
– nonconformity of; magic – including witchcraft; poor –
rates and duties; school – teaching; sex – various sexual
offences; slander – all verbal abuse; swearing – all profane
swearing. It has emerged from the analysis of several
different parishes in Essex and Cumbria that all the
ecclesiastical business in the various courts can be
organized under less than forty headings. A number of these
overlap with those devised for other courts. As with most
courts, there are occasionally longer personal depositions.
These cannot be dealt with in the fashion described above.
They need to be fully transcribed and kept intact, with
cross-references to them by name and subject.

3:10 *Quarter Sessions.*

Quarter Sessions records are of very many different
kinds, but one of the most interesting is the presentment.
An example of such a record is given in chapter 2. The cards
generated for our indexes differ only in colour from those
used for court leet cases. As with other court records, one
copy is kept under the source, each name is abstracted onto
a small white name index card, which gives the name, a brief
description of the role of the individual and the type of
case, and source and date. One copy of the original is cut
up and put into the subject index under such headings as
alien – harbouring of; doctrine – nonconformity of; fraud;
licence – to practice in various occupations; magic
–including witchcraft; sex – various offences; trespass –

on property. It will be seen that these overlap with the categories devised for the previous courts we have considered. On the basis of extensive work on the Quarter Sessions records for Essex and Cumbria it would seem that, once again, between thirty and forty subject categories would encompass all the types of case that occurred in this court. We also put one copy in a 'court' index under the name of the accused.

3:11 Assize.

A full Assize deposition has already been illustrated above. The case is included not only because it represents the very large classes of central records which have rarely been used by local historians, but also because it constitutes one of the most lengthy and complex types of legal documents. Such depositions occur in most of the courts, whether they are ecclesiastical, Quarter Sessions, Assizes, Star Chamber, and they pose a special problem for any indexing system. In fact, they cannot really be re-ordered to make them fit neatly onto cards. We abstract relevant details from them for all of our indexes and use the full transcript when necessary.

3:12 Hearth Tax.

The taxation records for most periods are usually much briefer and more structured than most other classes of records and pose no especial problems. The top typed copy is kept in a file by source, by the date of the particular tax, while the first carbon copy is cut up and each name is glued onto a small gold card so that it will fit into the general name index. Thus each entry is roughly similar in size, if less complex, than the names in a parish register.

3:13 Will.

Wills have to be treated in much the same way as court depositions. They are usually long and detailed, and the document needs to be examined as a whole. For this reason we do not make numerous copies but have developed another system of indexing them which we find useful. A special will abstract form is illustrated as figure 3:11.

It will be seen that at the top of each small section the person to whom the reference or bequest is made is indicated, with his or her relationship to the testator or role in the will shown below. The details of any bequest are placed next, and at the bottom of each 'box' is the name of the will-maker and the date it was made. The top copy is kept intact, and filed alphabetically with the other wills under the name of the testator so that the wills for any individual or family can easily be found. The next copy, which is on pink paper, is cut up so that each 'box' forms a card of suitable size for the name index. The name of the will-maker himself has to be written on another pink card, with date of making, reference, and proving date, otherwise his name would not be incorporated in the name index. Another copy is filed in the subject index. Wills frequently contain bequests to the church, to the poor, to godchildren and others, and sometimes have an interesting religious formula at the start.

3:14 Probate inventory.

As has already been stated, the probate inventories for Essex are, for the most part, lost. In the case of the very extensive Cumbrian inventories, they have been treated somewhat like depositions, in other words, a full copy of the original is kept, to which various indexes refer. At present, this copy is kept in the form of the original xerox

Figure 3:11. Will abstract form.

Interesting religious preamble		
D/ACW 12/160 Hen.ABBOT of Earls Colne, yeoman. (signature) 6/11/1625		
Robt.ABBOT $\frac{1}{3}$@ E S customary T. in Church Street, EC, with garden & 2 crofts of 3a., now in tenure & occ'n. of son Hen. - on condition that he pays wife £4 p.a. as long as she remains a widow Hen.ABBOTT 6/11/1625	Hen.ABBOT $\frac{1}{3}$@ E S in tenure & occ'n. of cust. T in Church Street left to son Robt. Hen.ABBOTT 6/11/1625	Thomazin ABBOT $\frac{1}{3}$@ E "beloved" W annuity or yearly rent of £4 from son Robt., while a widow Hen.ABBOTT 6/11/1625

Grace ABBOT
                              D
 	
£100 within 6 months of death
 	
Hen.ABBOTT 6/11/1625
	Francis WRIGHT husb/Grace
	                    bro-in-law
	
	5/- within a month of death
	
	Hen.ABBOTT 6/11/1625
		Grace WRIGHT w/Francis
		                              Z
		
		10/- within a month of death
		
		Hen.ABBOTT 6/11/1625

Robt.CROW (signature) W Hen.ABBOTT 6/11/1625	Dan.LEA (signature) W Hen.ABBOTT 6/11/1625	Wm.ADAMS jun. (signature) W (scribe) Hen.ABBOTT 6/11/1625

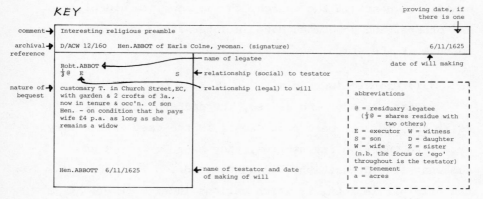

KEY

proving date, if
there is one

comment→ | Interesting religious preamble

archival→ | D/ACW 12/160   Hen.ABBOT of Earls Colne, yeoman. (signature)   6/11/1625
reference

Robt.ABBOT ← name of legatee   date of will making
$\frac{1}{3}$@ E   S ← relationship (social) to testator

nature of→ customary T. in Church Street,EC, ← relationship (legal) to will
bequest   with garden & 2 crofts of 3a.,
           now in tenure & occ'n. of son
           Hen. - on condition that he pays
           wife £4 p.a. as long as she
           remains a widow

```
abbreviations

@ = residuary legatee
  ($\frac{1}{3}$@ = shares residue with
       two others)
E = executor   W = witness
S = son        D = daughter
W = wife       Z = sister
(n.b. the focus or 'ego'
throughout is the testator)
T = tenement
a = acres
```

Hen.ABBOTT 6/11/1625 ← name of testator and date
                         of making of will

copy though a typed transcript will be necessary when extensive work on this source starts. These originals are filed
alphabetically.

3:15 Listing.

The listing for 1695 illustrated above contains highly
structured information. We type copies, incorporating
numbers to preserve the name order in the document. We index
it under each name, filling in all the kinship relationships
for each individual. Since the listing is such a central
document where it exists, it was also decided to make a special listing name index for the whole parish of Kirkby
Lonsdale.

3:16 Conclusion.

The method outlined above describes the analysis of
only a dozen representative sources; it can be extended on
the same principles to cover almost all historical sources
bearing on particular parishes. When extended, it will
gradually create indexes and cross-references which make it
possible to do justice to the richness and complexity of the
documents. The original sources will, in many cases, be
available as a photographic copy. A restructured but full
copy will be available by source; one will thus be able to
look up all the events in a particular period under a
particular date. On the basis of the work conducted so far,
it would appear that less than one hundred subject headings
will deal with the very great majority of the topics
encountered in the documents. Finally, a complete name index
will have been created. Every mention of an individual in
any type of document will finally come together in this
index. Using coloured cards to indicate quickly the

different classes of sources, retrieval of individual life histories will be possible. In essence, this name index is really a matter of taking the method of 'family reconstitution' one stage further by connecting all the references in other documents to those from the parish registers.

Chapter 4

THE QUALITY OF THE DATA

4:1 Too early for proper tests.

Until all the material has been collected and fully
indexed, it is impossible to give an accurate assessment of
how good the data is. Yet it would clearly be unwise to
attempt a project which could take a number of years without
being certain that the records are of a suitable quality.
We have already seen that in terms of sheer bulk, there is
a great deal of information. Two of the major queries which
remain are, firstly, whether this material only relates to
a limited section of the population under observation, for
example omitting the poorer and more mobile, and, secondly,
whether there are enough clues bearing on specific
individuals, properties, or subjects, to make it possible
to undertake a really worthwhile analysis. If the records
are spread too thinly or are too difficult to link together,
then we may still end up with an impoverished picture. A
more technical doubt will also trouble historians, namely,
what can we deduce from certain documents; in other words,
what do the documents really mean? The problem is familiar
in the context of parish registers where there are
difficulties when inferring birth dates from baptisms, but
it occurs in every form of record. For example, can we infer
residence in a certain place from certain types of documents, or can we infer guilt from certain types of accusa-

tion in court records? The pages below can only give a
preliminary and impressionistic answer to these doubts,
based on our progress up to the present. It is hoped that
it will be possible to devote a later volume to carrying
these tests further.

4:2 *The quality of specific sources: an example.*

One of the major technical problems is that even before
asking complex questions, a considerable amount of work
needs to be done checking what exactly the various sources
mean. During the stage of locating and transcribing documents it will have been necessary to learn a good deal about
the way in which the sources came into existence. The
history and nature of parish registers, procedure in a manor
court, methods of trial in the ecclesiastical and other
courts, these and other topics will have been absorbed. As
indicated above, there are many descriptions of such records
and how to use them. Yet it is not until all the records for
a particular area have been collected together that we can
begin to obtain an idea of the particular biases and gaps
in our knowledge. The proportion of the total population of
a given area which appears in a certain type of record, in
other words the criteria upon which a sample has been taken
from the total universe, cannot be established on the basis
of one, or even two, records. The degree of accuracy of each
source, and also the degree to which we can use its information as a measure of other things, cannot be estimated by
the use of one document. Only when several sources have been
indexed in the manner suggested in the previous chapter can
the biases and implications be established. For example, by
comparing parish registers with a listing of inhabitants or
a census, it is possible to discover to what extent each

source is selective (in omitting certain sections of the population) or inaccurate (in giving incorrect information even when people are included) or misleading (in appearing to give information on a topic which is not really dependable). Or again, we could compare probate inventories with Hearth Taxes, to see the biases in both these conventionally used indexes of wealth. A simple example may be given to show how the addition of several sources makes clear the bias or inadequacy of any one source: see figure 4:1.

The starting point is the 1695 listing for Lupton which gives the entry 'Joseph Tomlinson husbandman and his wife'. One might have thought that he was newly married or childless and one would not have known his wife's name. In the following year Joseph made a will which mentions six children and other relatives. If we look at the parish register for the parish of Kirby Lonsdale within which Lupton was situated, four of the six children in the will are mentioned; but we also discover two other children who are not mentioned in the will, either because they died before it was made, or were born after its making. Even after using these sources there are still numerous gaps, for instance the baptisms of the later children and Joseph's parents deaths. These are partially filled in by the parish register for Sedbergh, a town six miles to the north-east of Lupton.

Another way of illustrating these general points is to take one specific document, representative of a class, in order to see how much we can learn about its composition and meaning from placing it alongside other material. Let us consider the views of frankpledge. A great deal has been written about these views in general, but very little indeed

Figure 4:1. The superimposition of records.

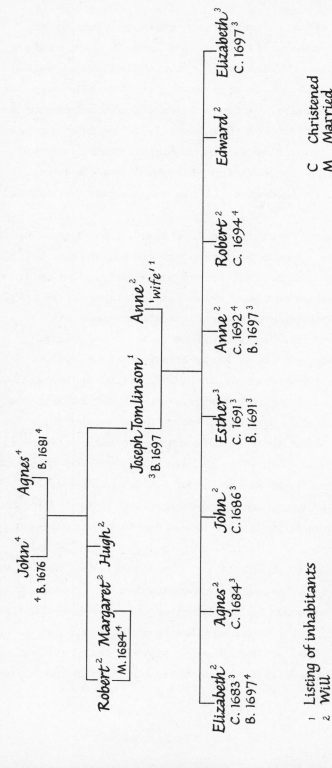

C   Christened
M   Married
B   Buried

1   Listing of inhabitants
2   Will
3   Parish register of Kirkby Lonsdale
4   Parish register of Sedbergh

is known about how they worked in practice. This is a
serious deficiency for, as stated earlier, they appear to
provide long lists of inhabitants and owners of property in
a number of English villages from the thirteenth century
onwards. If we were absolutely certain of the universe of
persons from which these documents selected and the various
biases they contain, they could provide the basis for a
great deal of social and demographic work. One of the
hardest facts to establish in historical parishes is whether
a person is alive or dead and whether he is still thought
to be resident in a certain place. These annual lists could
go a considerable way towards solving some of these
difficulties.

The general theory as to when these 'views' should be
held, who should appear, the age and other criteria of those
appearing can be summarized as follows. According to
Hearnshaw (1907: 17), the view of frankpledge has its
origins in the Sheriff's tourn. Basing himself on Maitland's
earlier analysis he states that all men of the lower orders
were required to place themselves in groups, usually of ten
or twelve, who were mutually responsible for one another's
good behaviour. In order to see that this system worked,
that is to see that youths as they attained the age of
twelve were duly enrolled, and to receive a report from the
tythingmen concerning the behaviour of the men under their
police supervision, the sheriff of the county, from Henry
II's time, if not before, twice a year went on tour ... and
held a specially full meeting of the hundred court, at which
he took the 'view of frankpledge'. At the same time there
were many private lords who claimed jurisdiction over their
tenants and the right to hold views of frankpledge. To have
a *curia cum leta* was not only to have exemption from

attendance at the sheriff's tourn but to hold a co-ordinate
court, drawing the same profit in fees and fines for the
sole benefit of the lord and not the king.

Suit at court, and thus appearance in the view of
frankpledge in person, was required from all called as
jurors in the court leet, all village officers among whom
chief pledges are often mentioned, and all persons between
the ages of twelve and sixty who have lived within the
precincts of the leet for a year and a day. Those who failed
to appear were amerced (put in mercy) as defaulters, while
those who were genuinely unable to attend sent an
'essoiner' with their excuse for absence. In general, women,
children, and nobles were not included in this rule though
evidence from the rolls suggests that many did attend and
were fined for non-appearance. The court leet with the view
of frankpledge was held not more than twice a year. The
sheriff's tourn was bound to be held at an accustomed spot,
but the manorial leets could be held anywhere within their
precincts. Personal summons was unnecessary and public
proclamation in the market place or church was all that was
demanded, with six to fifteen days notice most commonly.

By the sixteenth century, the Sheriff's tourn had been
reduced to the status of a communal leet, the tithing
systems seem to have almost disappeared, but the manorial
court leets remained and may even have been strengthened by
the sale of monastic lands and the encouragement from above
that they punish certain statutory offences. By then, the
view of frankpledge had taken the form of an oath of
allegiance to the king, but it seems that the same groups
were still bound to appear and to be amerced for non-
appearance (Hearnshaw 1907; Maitland 1889).

To see what happened in practice we may look at one

particular view in one Essex manor in one year. Part of the
view of frankpledge held for the manor of Earls Colne in
1590 is illustrated above (figure 2:6). The full view
records the names of some 80 persons of whom we know that
60 were residents in Earls Colne. We know that the total
population of the township was between 1,000 and 1,200 and
that this particular manor covered a little over half the
parish. If we estimate that there were roughly 500 males in
the parish, of whom 300 were aged over twelve, it would
appear that between one third and a half of the males aged
over twelve appeared in this view. As we shall see, the
proportion rises considerably if we combine several views
together.

We may wonder how much overlap there is between this
document and the parish registers for the parish, in other
words whether we can work out the proportions of those who
appear in the baptism, marriage and burial registers.
Unfortunately, the parish register only survives from 1558
and therefore it would only be possible to trace those aged
thirty years or younger. This partly explains the fact that
only three of the baptisms have been traced for the 60 Earls
Colne inhabitants - Henry Abbott junior was twenty-six, as
was Thomas Polley, and John Woodward was twenty-eight. By
comparing the view with a rental of 1589 for the same manor,
it is possible to establish one negative fact, that children
under twelve do not appear, even when they are the heirs to
property. Only investigation of later views, after a longer
run of parish registers, will establish whether a low
proportion of baptisms will ever be found because of the
high geographical mobility of the period.

The technique of family reconstitution requires that
before reconstituting a family it is necessary to find a

marriage; all families which do not have a marriage are
omitted. There have consequently been serious worries about
the unreconstitutable section; is it a minority, is it very
different from the reconstituted section? It will be
possible to answer these queries by combining parish
registers with other documents. For the 60 inhabitants of
Earls Colne named in this view, it is possible to discover
the marriages of 24; in other words, the reconstitutable
portion is a minority, consisting of some two-fifths of the
view. Finally, we may wonder how many of the people who are
named are mentioned in the burial register. An added problem
here is that the burial register is defective and is missing
from the very year of the view in 1590 until 1610. Thus any
burials in the next 20 years would be missing in any case.
Nevertheless, it is possible to discover the names of 23 of
the persons in the view in the burial register, which
indicates that linking with burials is easier than linking
with marriages or baptisms. But what is even more
interesting is that it is possible to discover the deaths
of 21 of the others from sources other than the parish
register, for example from wills, manorial transfers, or
testamentary cases in the ecclesiastical courts. These are
not only a valuable check on under-registration in the
parish register, but help to fill in gaps caused by a defective register. In total, therefore, it is possible to find
the deaths or burials of three-quarters of the residents in
the view. It is probable that if there had not been a defective register, the proportion would have been even higher.

On several occasions it has been stated that 60 out of
80 of those named were residents in Earls Colne. It is
interesting that by combining local records it is possible
to take a list of names and state confidently which were

local inhabitants and which were outsiders who owned
property but did not live in the parish. For the 20 who did
not, it is usually possible to state where they did live;
for example, Christopher Isack, Robert Pearetrey, John
Prentice, and William Prentice, were all from Colne Engaine.
When a person merely appeared in manorial records, but there
are no court leet, ecclesiastical court, parish register or
other records relating to him, it is assumed that he is an
outsider. The clustering of other references, in other words
the fact that people either have none, or if they have one
they have several, helps to give confidence in this method
and also underlines the quality of the documents. The fact
that a quarter of those appearing in the view were outsiders
also helps to remind us that we are, to a certain extent,
dealing with an artificial population when we examine the
business of a manorial court, covering a much wider area
than a parish.

Another question which has never really been answered
is the extent to which people appear in views by virtue of
residence rather than ownership of property. This could be
answered if we knew whether any of those appearing did, in
fact, hold no property of the manor. By comparing the names
with court land transfers and rentals it is possible to show
that 15 of the 60 Earls Colne residents in the view, or one
quarter, held no property of the manor. This quarter,
appeared merely by virtue of the fact that they were residents and, probably, heads of households. Five of them were
listed separately as 'deceners and residents' in the list,
the rest appeared under 'essoin' or 'homage'. None appeared
in the list of 'tenants and deceners for default' nor among
the 'customary tenants'. The manorial officials, therefore,
were carefully keeping them apart. More generally, it is

clearly very important to establish that these lists do not
merely give us landholders, but also landless men who are
resident. They thus become more like a listing, and less
like a rental.

Looking at the view from the other way round, we may
wonder what proportion of those who actually held property
of Earls Colne manor at the time appeared in the view; in
other words, can the view be used as a cross-section of
property-holders in a particular year? In the very full
rental of 1589 for the manor, there are some 78 persons
holding property in the manor. If we look at the views of
frankpledge for Earls Colne during the period 1587-92 we
find that 52, or two-thirds, appear in one or more of them.
If we then examine the 26 who do not appear we find that in
every case there is a good reason why they should not have
appeared. For instance, in a number of cases they only held
property for a few months; in other cases they were
represented in the views by other people. It thus seems safe
to say that several views of frankpledge combined will give
an almost total coverage of the customary tenants of the
manor. Of course, the freeholders will not appear, except
as residents within the precincts.

The views seldom give occupations, but it is possible
by combining them with other records to work out a rough
idea of the occupational structure year by year. In the 1590
view, we can establish the occupations of 55 out of 80 of
the persons, or 42 out of 60 of the residents. It would thus
seem that when all local records are taken into account, it
should be possible to establish the occupation/status of
about three-quarters of the resident adult males. In this
view, we find for example, 14 'yeomen', 6 'husbandmen', 4
'labourers', 4 butchers, 4 bakers/brewers, and a number of

other occupations including chapman, tilemaker, shoemaker, carrier, and shearman. Although there is ambiguity and overlap of occupations, and conflict between documents, it is encouraging that so much can be learnt. One interesting finding is that status seems to be given as higher in very localized documents, and to drop as the record moves to a national level. Thus while a Quarter Sessions roll may call a man a labourer, he will often be styled as a husbandman or yeoman in a will or manor court.

The enrolled views were very structured documents and it is intriguing and important to discover whether they followed any particular order. In the township of Lupton in Kirkby Lonsdale, for example, they are known to have followed house order so that it is possible to work out from each list where the individuals concerned lived. Figure 4:2 is a map of Earls Colne Street, based on one made in for 1598, which shows where some of the 60 residents in 1590 probably lived. The numbers on the map represent the order in the 1590 view, some of which is reproduced as figure 2:6. The map indicates that a large proportion of the Earls Colne residents appeared in the view for that year. We found that there is no street order in the view. It is possible that the draft lists contained some geographical order, but this had been lost by the time they were copied into the court roll. It seems more likely that each view was copied from the last one, with appropriate emendations, for certain 'blocks' of earlier views appear in later ones almost unchanged. This matter can be investigated further if we turn to the question of overlap between views.

To take one view of frankpledge in isolation, as we have done above, is to underestimate their value. Not only are there two manors in the parish, which complement each

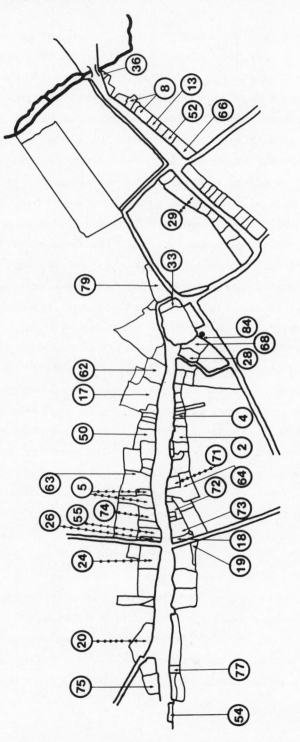

Figure 4:2. Map of residence of those in the 1590 view.

The numbers represent the order in the view, which is reproduced as figure 2:6.

•••••• Unsure, or sub-tenanted, holdings.

other, but views were sometimes held more than once a year. Furthermore, it is possible that a separate section of tenants and residents were called at each view. If this were the case, and it was accepted that it was a person's duty to appear not at every view but once in a while, in order to estimate what proportion of the adults in a village appeared, it would be necessary to take a set of views as a whole. This has been undertaken for a series of seven views taken for Earls Colne manor from July 1587 to June 1593, in other words the six years which encompass the 1590 view we have been analysing. In these seven views there are 172 persons mentioned in all. Thus the 80 we have been examining represent less than half of those who appeared during these six years. Furthermore, a graph of total attendance at the views shows that these six years saw lower than average attendance: see figure 4:3. During these six years, an average of 65 names was recorded, while in the slightly later period there was an average of 80 names. It

Figure 4:3. Attendance at views of frankpledge.

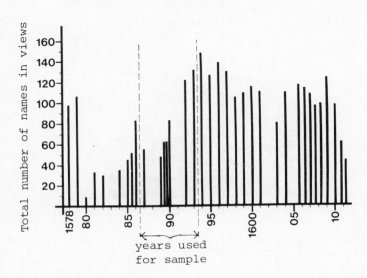

can be seen that we have not chosen the best documented period.

Perhaps the most difficult, yet most intriguing, problem is the degree to which the number of persons appearing in these views over a period of years was greater than the 80 suggested for the one sample year. That this is likely to be so is indicated by the fact that in the seven sample views from 1587 to 1593, the mean average number of attendances was 2.5 per person. Unless we assume that this was the average length of time a person lived in Earls Colne, or held property there, it would seem that people only appeared in some courts. This would suggest that a much larger proportion of the adult population would appear at some point or other. Combined with Colne Priory manor court, it would be possible to argue that the record provides a good coverage of a large proportion of adult males. A preliminary estimate of the dimensions of overlap may be given.

Figure 4:4. Life history of Henry Abbott of Earls Colne.

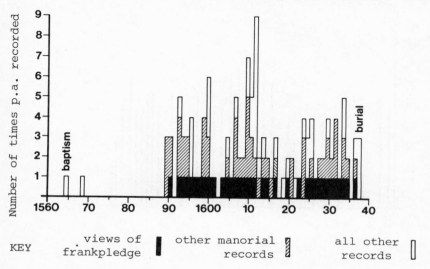

There was one very brief and short view in 1589; if we exclude this one, there were 12 persons only who appeared in all of the views for the six years. This is one half of those whom one knows from other sources were resident throughout the period and appeared in one or other view. This indicates the way in which people were dropped from the views, even though resident. Another finding is that of the 58 persons who appeared in the July 1587 view, some 21 also appeared in 1593 view. Although this is a very rough suggestion that about half of those who lived or held property had disappeared in six years, it does fit with what we know of the high geographical mobility of the period and does indicate the way in which these records could help to document such mobility in great detail. With an average list of about 65 per year, it will be seen that between one third and one half were new each year. Whether we take this as an index of land purchase or residence, it suggests an enormous turnover of population, the causes and exact dimensions of which will require further investigation. Of 58 in the first view, 11 did not appear again, none only appeared in the second view, 9 appeared only in the third view, 6 only in the fourth. Thus it would seem that perhaps between one-sixth and one-tenth of the frankpledge appeared only once and that this temporary appearance would account for between one-third and one-half of the change from year to year.

Finally, detailed work on reconstituting individual life-histories from all available records has tended to give confidence in these documents. It has indicated that the evidence from the two sets of documents correspond. When other documents show that a person moved into the parish, he starts to appear in the views; when he stops appearing altogether, other records also cease and it is clear that

he has either left or died. One example of this may be
given: see figure 4:4.

The importance of this is that it means that we can use
these records to establish whether a person is resident in
a certain year, or whether he has left. For a number of
demographic, social and economic questions it is essential
to know the dimensions of the universe of persons one is
sampling from, and in the absence of a census this is
usually impossible. Although inferior to repetitive
listings, the views of frankpledge or other lists of
customary tenants, extending in some manors from the fourteenth to eighteenth centuries, provide a unique source for
overcoming some of the problems.

4:3 The visibility of ordinary people in the past.
The belief that little can be found out about ordinary
people in the past, in other words those below the level of
the gentry, still lingers on, enshrined in echoes of the
'short and simple annals of the poor'. R. H. Tawney provided
a brilliant analysis of the economic conditions of the
English sixteenth-century peasantry in general, but
concluded 'What manner of men these were in that personal
life of which economics is but the squalid scaffolding ...
we cannot say. Of the hopes and fears and aspirations of the
men who tilled the fields which still give us in due season
their kindly fruit, we know hardly more than of the Roman
plebs, far less than of the democracy of Athens. Yet these
men too had their visions. Their silence is the taciturnity
of men, not the speechlessness of dumb beasts' (1912: 121).
There are two separate questions which need to be answered.
The first is, how many people entirely escaped being
recorded at all in historical documents and who were they?

The second is implied by Tawney, namely, even if we know
about one aspect of a person's life, for example his
economic position in a particular tax document, are we
likely to be able to piece together other aspects so that
we can begin to probe beyond the material world into the social and mental? A further complication is that it may be
argued that individuals in the past were so geographically
mobile that it is unlikely that we will catch more than a
fleeting glimpse of a specific person as he or she passes
through a particular place, tantalizing but unrewarding.

The worry about the 'invisible part of the iceberg'
must have assailed many historians and they are not usually
in a position to overcome it. Bringing together a number of
different sources can partly solve the problem. If it is the
case that when we have accumulated all possible references
to people in the past, it turns out that there are numerous
individuals who only appear once, we may well suspect that
there are considerable numbers who failed to make even this
one chance appearance, although living in a particular
community for a number of years. If, however, it turns out
to be the case that where there is one reference to a
person, there tend to be several references, there are some
grounds for believing that most people will have been
recorded. It appears that a number of sources intersected
and if a person was missed by one, he would probably be
picked up in another.

One way of approaching the problem is to see how many
people who appear in one kind of village document also
appear in others. For example, for the 60 people in the view
of frankpledge for whom there is no evidence that they lived
outside Earls Colne, we can subsequently discover by
checking them against the local records that all of them

appear to be mentioned in several other types of document. This suggests that the chance that a person will escape altogether is fairly slight.

Yet it is clear that the only way to establish beyond doubt that we are not just observing the historically visible minority, is to obtain a list of people who are known to have been resident in a community at a point in time, a list which is separate and distinct from the normal types of historical documents which survive. The fairly numerous informal listings of inhabitants for the pre-nineteenth century may be used to check the coverage of other documents in this way, and some attempts have been made to use them for this purpose, for instance in an early article by Styles (1951-2). But even listings are only one, rare, variety of local record. It is very difficult to obtain an independent list of inhabitants. Three such checklists can be constructed for Earls Colne in the seventeenth century, however. The first is based on the Account Book kept by the lord of the manor. During the period 1603-31, Richard Harlakenden noted down the names of over 280 persons in the Account Book. They were mentioned in numerous contexts, from the builder and bricklayer who worked for him to lawyers and informants in court cases. It is clear from the document that about 80 of these were living outside Earls Colne, of the remaining 200, a few are referred to so vaguely that it is impossible to identify them. But we may wonder how many of the rest are never mentioned in any other local record. The answer, is four persons at the most, and even some of these may have not been inhabitants.

The second checklist is provided by the Diary of Ralph Josselin, who was vicar of the parish and resident from 1641 to 1683 (Macfarlane 1976a). In this diary he mentions 195

people who lived for more than a few weeks in Earls Colne
while he was vicar. These seem to have been spread right
across the social range and to have included the migratory
as well as the settled, the very poor as well as the very
rich. We may wonder what proportion of these people passed
through the community, noted by Josselin, but invisible in
other records. At present 14 of those he mentions cannot be
definitely identified, either because Josselin gave no
forename, or because he gave too few details to make it
possible to distinguish between several people who shared
that forename/surname in the parish at the time. If we
include these among the persons for whom we do have
references in other documents, albeit ambiguous ones, we are
only left with 5 out of 195 persons, or less than 2.5%, who
leave no trace in other records. Furthermore, we can specify
exactly who they were. They were all Josselin's own hired
servants, present in the village for one or two years, and
aged between fifteen and twenty-two. On the basis of this
sample, it would appear that only a tiny fraction of a
seventeenth-century community was invisible, and this portion consisted of young servants. It is of course dangerous
to generalize for earlier and later periods, but at the
present there are no grounds for believing that the records
for the hundred years before Josselin are worse in terms of
documentation than the mid seventeenth century. It would
seem, therefore, that from the mid sixteenth century we are
dealing with an almost universally recorded population.

One final checklist is provided by the list of people
who signed the oath of loyalty to William and Mary, known
as an 'Association Roll' in 1696. This is particularly full
for Earls Colne and contains 160 male names. Four names are
unreadable but of the 156 other names all but 6 appear in

some other document. These other documents suggest that the
list contains a cross-section of the parish from rich to
poor and from young to old. It is therefore comforting to
find less than 5% of those listed go unrecorded in more
normal parish documents.

The second doubt raised above was whether, even if
people appear at least once, they would tend to generate
enough other records to make it possible to piece together
a number of facets of their lives. Although based on only
preliminary and partial workings, it is possible to give
some hints as to the depth of data on the basis of the lists
of persons from the sources which have already been
discussed. If we take the 1590 view of frankpledge first,
it would appear that of the 60 residents in the parish, we
can establish an occupation or status for three-quarters,
we can place over half in the exact house in which they were
living, we can establish whether they held land, and, if
they did, the precise nature of their holdings. Perhaps most
impressive of all is the evidence concerning their moral
behaviour in the church courts. Of the 60 persons in the
view, we only know for certain that 5 did not appear in the
archdeaconry or consistory courts at some point in their
lives. The other 55 appear in the records and it is possible
that 1 or 2 of the remainder will appear when further
ecclesiastical records have been searched. Two of those were
labourers, and another 2 who did not appear were only in the
parish for a short period, Robert Lysse for seven years,
Benjamin Handler for four. Further work on court leet and
other court records will establish how large a proportion
appear in other legal records. It is clear, however, that
a good deal can be learnt about the social and economic
position of a large proportion of those listed in the view

of frankpledge.

Although we have seen that a number of those who appeared in the view of frankpledge were small landless men, it could be argued that there is some bias towards the richer and less mobile in both this record and the Account Book. We may therefore turn to the 195 Earls Colne inhabitants mentioned by Josselin. The very great amount that can be found about most of them is indicated in the biographies and maps appended to the edition of the Diary.

These were constructed on the basis of a partial manual index of some of the local documents. Even so, it is possible to build up a fairly full picture of most of those whom Josselin mentions. The information one can find can be summarized as follows. Taking a rough sample of 50 of the men and 25 of the women Josselin mentioned, it is possible to find the burial date of three-quarters of the men and half the women, the baptism of half of the men and one-third of the women. One-half of the men and one-sixth of the women (who included servants) were both baptized and buried in the parish. Of those people one could identify unambiguously, it was possible to place approximately three-quarters in a specific house in the village by using contemporary maps and making the assumption that if a person owned one house and was known to live in the village, he or she would live in that house rather than elsewhere. When full reconstruction is completed, it does not seem overoptimistic to believe that one will be able to place over 80% of individuals at any point in time in the houses where they were residing. As regards occupation or status, it is possible from various records to obtain explicit statements concerning the position of over half those men mentioned by Josselin, and by implication and inference of a further quarter. Furthermore,

there is a vast amount of information in the documents
concerning landholding, so that it is possible to say fairly
exactly what lands and other properties were held by up to
three-quarters of those who can be identified.

Turning to non-economic variables, we may wonder what
we can learn about kinship and marriage. In well over half
of the cases of identified individuals, the forename and
surname of both parents are recoverable. Kinship diagrams
of several generations depth could be drawn for these and
some of the other individuals. It is almost always possible
to find out whether the individuals were married, though
often this fact and the name of the spouse has to be
ascertained from sources other than the Earls Colne parish
registers. Because of the high rate of geographical mobility
between birth and marriage and the custom of marrying (and
hence registering) in the bride's parish and then settling
in the groom's, the proportion of people for whom one can
work out age at marriage is small. In only 6 out of the
sample of 50 men, and 6 of the 25 women, do we have both
baptism and marriage given in the Earls Colne register. It
is made plain that a satisfactory picture can only be
obtained by moving outside the parish.

Signatures or marks on wills and other documents enable
us to piece together evidence on the literacy of
individuals. From the various sources it is possible to work
out the signing ability of nearly one-half of the adults in
the Josselin sample. This is the case, despite the fact that
only a quarter of those who appear to have died in the
parish seem to have made wills. Evidence from the witnessing
of other wills, signatures on the very full late seventeenth-century Association Roll, as well as other sources
enable one to fill out the number of signatures.

Furthermore, wills and their introductory formulae are an
interesting, if deceptive, index of religious affiliation.
But even omitting this source, it is possible to find out
something about the religious behaviour of one-sixth of the
identified sample, without using Josselin's own remarks as
evidence. The ecclesiastical records are very poor in
comparison to those for the Elizabethan period, so that it
may be possible to say something about the religious position of a larger proportion of Elizabethan villagers. This
is suggested by the fact, mentioned above, that 55 out of
60 of the sample males in the 1590 view of frankpledge
appeared in the ecclesiastical records. Earlier records are
also fuller on sexual and other moral offences as well as
petty crime.

By correlating the various activities and roles which
have been briefly summarized above, for example religion
with wealth with literacy with kinship, it will be possible
to carry out work on the overlap of variables. It would seem
that there is enough information, from at least the mid sixteenth century in a well documented parish, for it to be
possible to undertake complex sociological and historical
work.

4:4 The quality of the data: places.

One of the main ways of classifying the extensive data
is by spatial distribution. Many of the most interesting
questions have not only a temporal but also a spatial dimension. It is partly for this reason that the various 'place'
indexes which we have described above were created. But
their success will obviously depend on the completeness and
accuracy of the registration of land ownership and occupation in the original documents. It is difficult to convey

an impression of how good the material for Earls Colne is
in this respect. Perhaps some hint of the quality may emerge
from the fact that it is possible to trace every single
field and every house and its ownership from a detailed map
of the parish made in 1598 up to 1854 by way of the 1838
tithe award map. Furthermore, it is possible to trace the
fields back into the fifteenth century at least. It is
therefore possible to know exactly who owned every one of
the roughly 650 separate parcels of property, land or
housing, at any point during the last four hundred years.
The quantity of material bearing on even the smallest plot
is quite staggering. If we confine ourselves to just one
house, that which is transferred in the manorial document
described in the last chapter, namely a tenement in Church
Street, the amount of information that can be found out is
as follows.

The situation of the house is illustrated in figure
4:5; the shaded lands were usually transferred with it. In

Figure 4:5. Tenement in Church Street.

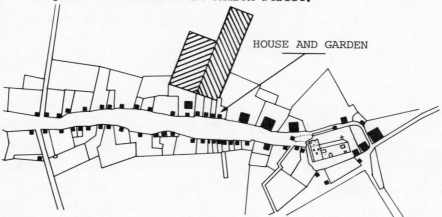

HOUSE AND GARDEN

Passed with the house from 1530 to 1819,
when they were split off

about 1500 a rental mentions that the house was held by
Isabel Tedyr at the rent of 16d.; in 1854 a quitrent for
this piece was still 1s. 4d. It is probably possible to go
back to 1380 in the court rolls. Between 1500 and 1841 there
are numerous transfers of the property, many of them more
detailed than the sample one quoted above. Among them are
descriptions in at least twenty-one separate documents. The
property ended up in the hands of Samuel Sadd, whose
household is described in the Census of 1851. One can, in
these descriptions, fill in the ownership, exact position,
size, rent, etc. from year to year. The same is true of most
of the property in the parish. It is of course not possible
to deduce who was actually residing in the property at all
times, for only a small proportion of the documents give the
name of the occupant as well as the owner. Yet it is
possible to draw up maps of ownership for almost any year
from about 1550 to the present.

4:5 *The quality of the data: families.*

The owners of the tenement in Church Street described
above, during the period 1530-1730, were the Abbott family,
who were present in the village for a few years on either
side of the above dates. We may look at this family in more
detail to see how much can be learnt about them. The cards
for this family constitute perhaps one-sixhundreth of the
total 50,000 cards in the index in March 1977 (the name
index will finally be about twice that size). We are
therefore dealing with a very small fraction of the total
families. The Abbotts were chosen because they were the
first reasonably sized family in the first box, starting
with the letters AB.

The study of kinship, marriage and the family is one of

Figure 4:6. Kinship diagram of the Abbott family.

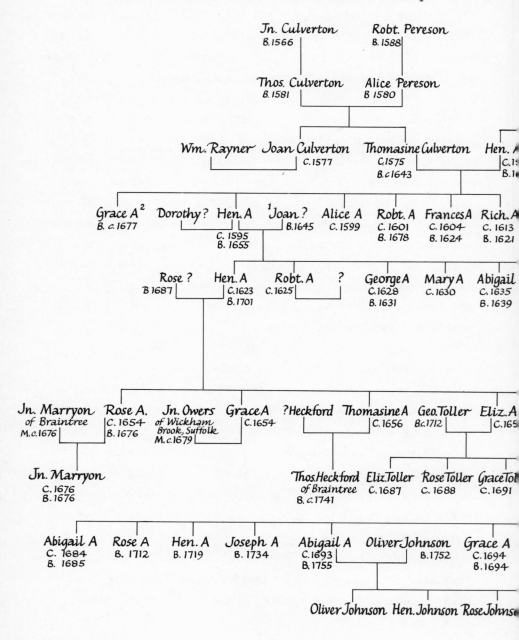

Figure 4:6, continued.

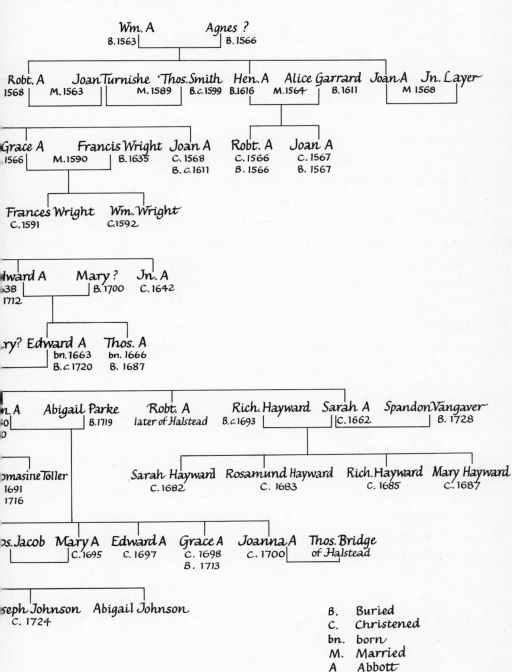

B.   Buried
C.   Christened
bn. born
M.   Married
A   Abbott

the central concerns of social anthropology and sociology,
and the preliminary is to know who a person's kin were. Is
it possible on the basis of local records to reconstruct
genealogies? The one we have reconstructed for the Abbott
family is shown as figure 4:6. This diagram was constructed
by hand, on the basis of an analysis of only part of the
data. It is likely that it will be improved in the future.
Yet it already illustrates that a very considerable amount
can be learnt about our sample family from local records.
Among the interesting points to note is the fact that only
four of the marriages were found in the local parish
register; thus only a small part of the family would have
been reconstitutable by family reconstitution. Yet, by
combining records, it is possible not only to construct the
genealogy, but to work out the date and names in marriages
for which we have no direct records. It is also worth
remarking that the diagram matches in detail, and exceeds
in generational depth, most of the kinship diagrams which
it is possible to construct from contemporary anthropological investigation.

   4:6 The quality of the data: individuals.
   It is probable that an equally good vignette could be
built up of any of the male Abbotts in the kinship diagram
above, extending over a period of two hundred years. For the
purposes of exposition, we may take just one individual,
Henry Abbott the second. A shortened literary account of the
life and relationships of this one man would read as
follows.
   Henry Abbott is an atypical inhabitant of Earls Colne
in so far as both his baptism and burial are noted in the
parish register and that he lived there for most, if not

all, of his seventy-three years. For this reason we have
more than average information about him and it becomes
possible to use him as a 'case study'.

He was baptized, son of Robert Abbott, on 26 March
1564. He was the first child of the marriage. His parents
had married the previous September so that he was the
product of a bridal pregnancy, though not one noted in the
ecclesiastical court. His mother's surname was Turnishe but
it is possible that she was a widow and that she was in fact
the sister of Robert Pereson of Earls Colne. Pereson is
mentioned in Robert Abbott's will as 'brother', a form often
used in contemporary wills for brother-in-law. We know that
Robert had an unmarried sister Joan, mentioned in his will,
and that Robert Pereson's wife was also a Joan. The
incidence of siblings having the same name is rare so we
conclude that he must have been referring to his wife's kin.
Unfortunately the parish register does not survive before
1559 so we have no means of proving this hypothesis. It is
an important link in the life of Henry Abbott and would help
to explain his marriage to an heiress aged only fifteen who
happened to be the granddaughter and ward of the same Robert
Pereson.

Robert Abbott died in 1568 leaving his son £6 13s.4d.
(he had no land) to be paid to him at the age of twenty-one.
He left his younger daughters, Grace and Joan, a similar
amount to be divided between them. Robert made his own
brother Henry (whom we shall refer to as Henry senior)
guardian of his son and trustee of the money, on condition
that he put in a sufficient bond to Robert Pereson for the
payment of the legacy. His daughters remained in the care
of their mother. There is some confusion about whether or
whom his wife remarried. Certainly a Joan Abbott married

John Layer three months after the death of Robert, but this may well have been his sister rather than his widow as there are no further links between Henry Abbott and the Layers. There is more evidence to suggest that she married a widower, Thomas Smith, much later in 1589, about the same time incidentally as her son married. Henry acted as both a witness to the will of Thomas Smith in 1599 and was left £3 by it. Our experience with wills suggests that money bequests are rarely left to any but kin and there is no hint that this is an unpaid debt. This leads us to believe that Thomas Smith's widow was indeed Henry Abbott's mother. There is a possibility that Henry's sister Joan had married Thomas Smith but we have some evidence that she died unmarried in 1611.

We learn nothing further about Henry Abbott until 1589 when he was twenty-five. Local records are singularly poor at recording much about children, apart from their baptisms or untimely deaths, until the later seventeenth century when the poor appear in apprenticeship indentures and settlement papers. There is no evidence to suggest that he moved from Earls Colne, but whether he lived with his mother or uncle, or in what house he lived, we cannot say. When he reappears he does so as a result of his marriage to Thomasine Culverton. There is no record of this in the Earls Colne register, and we have not been able to trace it to any of the surrounding parishes, but it must have occurred about 1589. In that year he is presented on three separate occasions for ditch offences in the manor court. We know that he held no land, neither did he inherit any until many years later, but he appears in the right of his wife who did hold land. She was the daughter of Thomas Culverton who died when she was only six years old. He left her and her younger

sister Joan in the custody of his father-in-law, the same
Robert Pereson. Each inherited quite sizable portions of
land, as well as goods, which they were to have at the age
of twenty-one or, as in this case, at marriage. One wonders
how much chance played a part in the marriage. Little would
seem to be the answer given the age difference between them,
the unusually young age of the bride, and the fact that they
both had the same guardian, indeed may have been brought up
together. For the subsequent history of the Abbott family
this marriage and the wealth it brought them seems to have
been most significant. During the next hundred years they
move from being landless to holding a good tenth of the
copyhold and freehold lands in Earls Colne, and by further
assiduous marriages, land all over north Essex and Suffolk.

We must assume, for want of evidence to the contrary,
that Henry was principally a farmer. We know however that
his son and grandson were both sayweavers and it is possible
that he was a weaver too. In one leet case the lord of the
manor apparently sent his bailiff to distrain cloth from him
for an amercement of £5 that had remained unpaid from an
earlier court. Henry is described as having scoffed at them
and alluded to the recent death of the lord's wife by saying
'I had thought your master had sent you to have taken cloth
to make mourning coats.' He described himself in his will
as a yeoman but this may have been the assessment of his
status in the village rather than a reflection on his
occupation.

The early references to him in the court leet give us
some idea of his character as seen through the eyes of the
lord of the manor, Roger Harlakenden. One gets the strong
impression from reading these that there was a feud between
them. We know some of the reasons why this might have been

the case. The manors of Earls Colne and Colne Priory were
first leased to Roger Harlakenden and then bought by him
from Edward, the Earl of Oxford. The Earl had been an
absentee landlord as had his family for generations. Their
Essex seat was at Hedingham Castle, though after their
purchase of the Priory lands they did use Colne Priory as
a dower house. Thus the inhabitants had been used to a lax
situation where the Earl's steward would come once or twice
a year to hold court and collect fines for admission to
copyhold property, perhaps amerce someone for a leet
offence, and then go away again. It seems that the
Harlakendens intended to resuscitate the manor courts and
to work them, whether just for their own financial advantage
or from a genuine desire to improve the morals and behaviour
of the inhabitants, we cannot say. There are reasons for
believing that both may be true. Certainly they were a
strongly puritan family. Roger's grandson, Richard, was
described as a 'saint' by a neighbouring vicar, Samuel
Rogers (Shipps), and Ralph Josselin's attitude would support
the idea that they were a 'worthy' family. On the other hand
there is plenty of evidence to show that they were efficient
businessmen. There was a long dispute with the heirs of
Edward, Earl of Oxford over the right to Colne Priory manor.
They accused Roger Harlakenden of having embezzled it from
the Earl who had never intended to sell it. This dispute was
still going on in 1640, at least fifty years after the
original sale. We also know that the Earl and Roger
Harlakenden fought over much less weighty issues. For
instance, Roger Harlakenden and some neighbouring gentry had
tried to replace the schoolmaster, William Adams, described
in a court deposition as 'a very unmeet man ... and also
very insufficient for his learning to instruct any children

in the latin tongue, and that by reason thereof divers youths had of a long space greatly lost their time to their hindrance' (REQ/271/76). Adams had retaliated by getting a patent from the Earl of Oxford who supported his case. He was not finally ousted until 1610.

We know that the villagers took sides in these disputes and that the Harlakendens depended on their own servants rather than their tenants to support them. There is no evidence that Henry Abbott ever appeared for the Earl, although his brother-in-law Francis Wright was involved in one case, but there is a strong hint that he was persecuted by Roger Harlakenden through his manor court. A document described in chapter 3 lists five offences said to have been committed by Henry, for which he was amerced the incredible sum of £5. That this was taken by distress has already been alluded to. In the latter case he is 'adjudged by the whole court a vile and troublesome member of the Commonwealth' for 'many bad and lewd misdemeanours'. Further weight was apparently given to the leet case by an endorsement in the court of King's Bench. It is interesting to note that a year before this case, Henry was accused in the ecclesiastical court 'that he was drunk and in his drunkennes he said that his privities or prick was longer by four inches than one Clerke's there passing'. He was dismissed on the evidence of the churchwardens who said that the detection was untrue, but one wonders whether this was the William Clark whose finger he wounded a year later. Over subsequent years he was further presented in the manor court for unlicensed tree cutting, for contempt of court, for converting barns into cottages without licence, for taking inmates and the usual array of unscoured ditch offences. In 1623, though, he was the first inhabitant to sign an agreement with the lord on

behalf of the tenants, for the right to cut timber on their
copyhold lands. He was by then nearly sixty years old and
seems to have become a respectable inhabitant. His first and
only village office was as an aleconder in 1625.

   A reason why he might have incurred the dislike of the
Harlakendens was for his religious 'non-conformity'. Apart
from the earliest presentment in the ecclesiastical court
for drunkenness, the majority of other appearances were for
church offences. For instance, in 1594 and 1595 he was
accused of refusing to pay the assessment for the reparation
of the church, then again in 1609 he was 'detected' for
refusing to pay the 3s.4d. for the same purpose. The most
telling years are those immediately following. At the same
court in 1609 he was detected by the churchwardens 'for his
great negligence in not frequenting his parish church in
divine service time upon the sabbath days, and also that he
doth seldom or never upon any sabbath day repair to evening
prayer but at such time he is walking up and down the fields
as we are credibly informed'. For this offence he was
ordered to confess his guilt in church after the second
lesson and to certify to the authorities that he had done
so. At this point one should note that this is exactly the
time that Richard Harlakenden, son of Roger and now lord of
the manor, was exerting his influence to oust William Adams,
not only as schoolmaster but also as vicar of Earls Colne.
In May 1609, Thomas Greenfield had presented his credentials
to the ecclesiastical court and had been appointed the new
vicar of Earls Colne. It was in the following September that
Henry was presented for not attending church. At the same
court, Moses Rowton of Earls Colne was accused of using
reproachful words against the vicar. By July 1610 the affair
had escalated to the Assize court where Henry was indicted

for having interrupted the sermon of Thomas Greenfield.
Although this document is mutilated, it does seen that Henry
was able to plead that the indictment was insufficient.
Certainly he does not appear in the gaol calendar. The
affair seems then to have gone back to the ecclesiastical
court with Henry 'detected' the following January 'for that
he refuseth to take his place according to the
churchwardens' appointment and he is ordered to sit in the
pew and stool where he was formerly placed by the
churchwardens'. In March and April 1611 it was presented
'that he doth commonly depart out of the church before the
end of sermons divers sabbath days and especially on 30th
September 1610 he in base and most filthy manner did make
mouths and wring his chaps at our minister in gross sort'.
Henry in mitigation said that on the day named he was
unwell, and that he was now reconciled to Mr Greenfield. It
is interesting to note the other actors in this drama. Both
Richard Harlakenden and his wife Margaret were themselves
presented in the ecclesiastical court in 1606 for not having
received communion since 1604. They alleged that the cause
of the presentment was Mr Adams himself as he refused to
minister to them. Presumably the final effort to dislodge
him dates from this time. William Adams and his family tried
to make Mr Greenfield's job impossible. For instance,
William himself besides the usual tactic of refusing to
receive communion, threatened to strike Mr Greenfield with
a pitchfork in the churchyard. His son 'lay along in the
church at the reading of the lesson and disturbed the
minister', and Joan, William's wife, was presented for vio-
lently throwing a stone at the vicar in the churchyard.
Francis Wright, Henry Abbott's brother-in-law, was presented
'for slandering our minister', and Grace Wright, Henry's

sister was presented with Margaret Woodward 'for giving out
bad speeches against our minister concerning his doctrine
delivered in our parish church in most rude and bad manner'.
One cannot help wondering whether this alliance between the
Adams and the Abbotts was functioning during the earlier
affair when William Adams was the victor, and whether some
of the animosity sensed between the Harlakendens and Henry
Abbott is rooted in the same larger conflict. Certainly the
Harlakendens had the victory on this occasion as not only
did William Adams lose his living, but also in 1611 another
schoolmaster was appointed.

We turn from conflict to land and family. Henry added
to his landholding once in his life. On the death of his
uncle, Henry Abbott senior, he inherited the house in Church
Street referred to in the analysis of a landholding in the
section above. This occurred in 1616. It is interesting to
note that although he held Colne Priory land, he never
appeared in the view of frankpledge for that manor but
continued to appear and occasionally to act as a homage
juror in Earls Colne manor court. One of our observations
has been that there is little likelihood of anyone appearing
in more than one leet, which bears out the general principal
repeated in many of the guides to keeping a court leet,
'Everyone is in some leet, and no one is in two leets'
(Kitchin in Hearnshaw 1907: 84). Henry Abbott surrendered
all his land together with his wife's land in 1623, to their
own use for their lives and for the longer liver of them,
and at the death of the longer liver to their son Henry and
his wife Joan. We have not found this son's marriage either
in the Earls Colne register or in any neighbouring one, and
we never know the maiden name of his wife. It must have
occurred about 1623 so that the land transfer may well have

been a form of marriage payment. Henry the son was baptized 9 June 1595 and was probably the eldest son. Of his siblings, we know that a surviving elder child was a daughter, Grace (mentioned in her father's will) and that there were two further sisters and two brothers, so six children in all. A son and two daughters died before their father made his will in 1625 (see sample documents for this will). It is interesting to note that in this will he bequeathed the house in Church Street to his younger son, Robert, when he had already surrendered the remainder to his elder son and wife. There is no further transfer in the manor court until his death when it seems that the will overrides the earlier transfer and Robert is admitted tenant after his mother's death.

There is some difficulty in ever placing Henry Abbott in a particular house in the village. His wife brought land to the marriage but no house. In his will he mentions that his son Henry occupies the house that he inherited from his uncle. Only one rental in 1638 gives a hint that he may have lived in one of the houses in Holt Street that his wife's sister, Joan, inherited. She married out of the village and clearly never lived there herself.

There are many references to Henry Abbott that add only a little to the picture of the man, so that they have not been dwelt on at length in this summary. There are references to him in a number of rentals and a terrier which confirm what we already know of his landholdings. There are the appearances or non-appearances in the views of frankpledge, on average once a year from 1590 to 1636. These help to confirm his actual presence in the village over this period. There are the taxation returns: Lay Subsidies 1599-1629 and Ship Money 1636, which give the impression

that his actual wealth remained static over the period. He
is invariably taxed at 8s. There are the obscure references
to him in the manor court and in wills as a witness through
which we see that he could sign his name. In all, there are
over one hundred references to him during his life in the
documents that we have looked at. In conclusion, we repeat
that he was unusual in that he lived in Earls Colne for so
long, but not in the amount of information that one could
produce on him in any particular year.

It will be seen from the vast amount of information on
this one man that it would be impossible to attempt a
biographical approach to the history of a community. Yet the
presence of these biographies makes various kinds of
analysis possible. Some of these will be illustrated in the
next chapter.

Chapter 5

SOME USES FOR THE DATA

The method described in previous chapters may be
applied to any area, rural or urban, large or small, for
which there are historical records. In order to illustrate
some of the questions which it is possible to answer using
such records, we will take the two contrasted examples,
namely the parish of Earls Colne in Essex and that of Kirkby
Lonsdale in Cumbria. Documents from these two areas have
already been used to illustrate previous chapters. The
parishes were chosen because they contain very good records
and because they provide a good contrast. The Essex parish
lies in lowland England, near London, the Cumbrian parish
in the upland, pastoral area, near the northern border.
Analysis of the two parishes also makes it clear that the
survival of records dictates the type of questions it is
meaningful to ask. Many of the questions can only be asked
of one or the other parish because they need a specific
source in order to make the answer possible. The choice of
samples circumscribes the analysis: it is limited to the
sixteenth to eighteenth centuries and to rural areas.

It is necessary to stress that the work on Earls Colne
and Kirkby Lonsdale is only now reaching a stage where it
is beginning to be possible to obtain answers to questions.
The following sections do not embody these answers, which
will be contained in other future publications. The evidence

cited from these villages is therefore impressionistic and
statistically largely meaningless. It is given to illustrate
some of the questions one might ask and some of the sources
one might use to answer them. This needs to be emphasized
strongly since it would be very misleading to give the
impression that the enormous investment of time in
accumulating data, and the richness of that data, has
culminated in the bare and somewhat insubstantial specula-
tions of this chapter. Almost every one of the topics raised
below would require a chapter or even a book to itself if
we were to deal with it properly, even at the level of the
two parishes. The necessity to survey most possible uses of
the data in a few thousand words leads to a superficiality
which those who are familiar with early modern English
history must pardon. Yet it does seem that a book
prescribing an arduous and time-consuming technique would
be deficient without some attempt to sketch in some of the
questions we could answer after the methodology had been
applied.

5:1 The physical background.

The previous chapter has shown that is is possible to
trace the site and ownership of particular fields and houses
over many hundreds of years. Combined with archaeological
fieldwork in the village, it is possible to date not only
buildings but also hedges and ditches. Hoskins, for example,
provides an account of the methods which may be used (1970).
One is able to build up maps of the parish at many points
in time and watch the landscape evolving. This is a level
which may be integrated with study of the soil and geology
of the region. The methodology for undertaking such work is
now well established and described. There are also other
features of the physical background within which past

inhabitants lived which may be explored.

One feature of the physical background which was of enormous importance was the weather. There is growing evidence of major climatic shifts during the sixteenth and seventeenth centuries. Hard winters and drought have been adduced to help explain the incidence of epidemics, for example (Appleby 1973). Information on the weather can usually only be gleaned indirectly from local records. The fluctuation of prices in inventories and account books, or fluctuations in burials, have to be used as an index, albeit distorted, of the weather. Sometimes a local inhabitant did jot down the major features as they appeared to him. An example of this is contained in the diary of an Earls Colne inhabitant, Ralph Josselin (Macfarlane 1976a). The major features of the weather in this Essex village over a forty-year period in the seventeenth century are illustrated by that document; fluctuations can be correlated with demographic and economic changes in considerable detail. The impact of the weather on the inhabitants would depend very considerably on the buildings, furniture and clothing used in the period.

Only in parishes where probate inventories have survived is it possible to study changes in household furniture. Thus, for example, if we look at the inventories made by the inhabitants of the chapelry of Lupton within the parish of Kirkby Lonsdale, a sub-part of the parish with approximately 150 inhabitants in the seventeenth century, we notice a gradual diversification of furnishings. Nearly 150 inventories for this tiny hamlet survive covering the period 1550-1720. In the two dozen pre-1600 ones items include kettles, pans, pots, cauldrons, pewter vessels, chests, chairs and other similar basic furnishings. In 1604

a silver spoon is mentioned, in 1608 a candlestick, in 1659
a cheese press, and in 1679 a clock and case. Given the
larger sample of 2,000 or so inventories for the whole
parish of Kirkby Lonsdale it would be possible to study in
some detail how houses were furnished, and how new standards
emerged.

Inventories also record details of clothing and changes
in the cost of garments. 'Rayment' or 'apparel' is often
listed separately and is mentioned as being worth 5s.4d.,
20s. and 13s. respectively in three late sixteenth-century
inventories for Lupton. Higher sums of 16s., 28s. and £2 are
mentioned in three seventeenth-century inventories. It would
be necessary in all such comparisons to know a good deal
about changes in the value of money and the exact status and
age of the deceased before interpreting comparisons. It
would be necessary to look at wider evidence to decide
whether the first mention of bodices and bands in 1636, or
'stockings' in 1679 reflected changing fashions, or was
merely a chance mention. The same precautions would need to
be taken if assessing changes in agricultural tools from
inventories.

Many other aspects of the physical background, which
must have conditioned the lives of Englishmen before the
industrial revolution, can be documented from local records.
Methods of heating and the collection of fuel can be studied
through inventories, account books and manorial records. The
supply of water and its regulation is often dealt with by
the local court leet which contains orders to prevent
contamination. The same source, as well as Quarter Sessions
records, deal with communication and transport. Every aspect
of the physical world, from hedges and ditches, cutting of
trees and undergrowth, to the upkeep of houses and the use

of land, was minutely regulated. In general, the physical
conditions within which people lived in the past can be
reconstructed in immense detail. This framework provides us
with an indispensible basis upon which to analyse more
abstract and impermanent features of the past.

5:2 *Economic life.*

The area in which English documents are richest is
economics. This is well known and consequently agricultural
and economic historians have for a long time drawn heavily
on local sources (Tawney 1912; Thirsk 1967). Shortage of
space forces us here to omit numerous topics such as land-
ownership and tenurial patterns, storage mechanisms, markets
and marketing, prices and currency, famines and scarcity,
taxation, gifts and exchanges. We will concentrate on eight
topics in a little detail.

The amount of capital invested in agricultural and non-
agricultural production may be investigated through the use
of inventories, wills, diaries, account books and manorial
records. At a simple level we can compare inventory totals.
If we take, for example, sixteenth-century inventories for
Lupton where animals are mentioned, we find that the mean
average value of the thirteen inventories of this kind made
by men was £40 if debts are excluded, £55 with debts. We may
compare this with the ten inventories of a similar kind made
between 1680 and 1689 in the same hamlet, where the mean
average value was £114, and the average when debts were
included £144. It is impossible, as yet, to be certain as
to the rate of inflation of currency in the period, but this
probably does indicate an increase in real value. The
comparisons become more precise if we compare particular
farms over the period and look at specific items. For

instance, in Lupton the Middleton family owned a farm called
Aikrigg Green. When it was inventoried in August 1586, the
goods, excluding debts, were worth £69 8s.4d., by September
1659 the goods were worth £272 3s.2d. excluding debts. On
this farm and others there then seems to have been a halt
in the rise in value of the movable goods in the later
seventeenth century. If we took the 2,000 inventories for
the whole parish, it would clearly be possible to work out
in some detail how much was invested in tools, animals,
seed, manure, loans and other items and then this could be
compared with the value of the land. It would be possible
to look at non-agricultural families to see how smiths,
tailors and other occupational groups compared in terms of
capital. It should be stressed that since many people,
particularly the aged, had already transferred a large part
of their wealth before they died to their children,
inventories can be a deceptive guide to capital.

In order to interpret the results of such an analysis
we need to know how many people were farmers, tailors etc.,
in other words we need to know something about the occupational structure. Although this can be pieced together from
other sources, the easiest way is through a listing of
inhabitants, though this only gives a cross-section at one
point in time. The listing for the chapelry of Lupton in
1695 named 137 persons. Thirty-five of these were said to
be 'husbandmen', one a yeoman and one a labourer; 16 persons
were of various trades, including a carpenter, a shoemaker,
a badger, a tailor, a miller, an innkeeper, a blacksmith and
a schoolmaster. This means that between a quarter and a
third of this apparently rural chapelry were primarily
engaged in non-agricultural occupations. That Lupton was not
exceptional in this can be seen if we compare it with the

listings for the other eight chapelries within Kirkby
Lonsdale; for example, in Killington to the north, of the
51 occupations of those not listed as 'pensioners', 12, or
a little under a quarter, were non-agricultural. These
included one or more of the following; miller, blacksmith,
tanner, spinster, cooper, weaver, cordwainer, skinner and
millwright. The survival of a listing makes it possible to
see whether such a large number of non-agriculturalists
would have been indicated by the inventories alone.
Excluding the inventories made for women, we would expect
to find about one-quarter of the 120 inventories to be made
for non-agriculturalists. In fact the number is a good deal
less. Inventories often give the occupation or status of the
deceased, but only five Lupton inventories mention non-
agricultural occupations: a tailor in 1680, waller in 1686,
tanner in 1688, carpenter in 1710 and blacksmith in 1712.
Four of these men left tools of their trade which were
inventoried, the tailor is the exception. None of the other
inventories contain special tools of trade, with the exception of hemp, yarn and cloth, which is mentioned in the
inventories of 13 other persons, most of whom are styled
'husbandmen'. Inventories as a source in this area would
therefore give a misleading impression of the amount of non-
agricultural specialization.

Any belief that we may have had that in England in the
seventeenth century everyone was solely engaged in agriculture, in a subsistence economy with little economic
specialization, would have begun to be undermined by the
analysis of the occupational structure. Furthermore, if this
diversification is found in the apparently remote Cumbrian
parish it is likely that the development of the market and
secondary industries would have proceeded even further in

the Essex parish. An examination of the land transmission
patterns of the two areas throws further light on the
subject. By the late sixteenth century in Earls Colne the
market in land was fully developed. Taking just one of the
two manors in the parish, Earls Colne manor, and looking at
the five-year period 1589-93, some 51 parcels of copyhold
property were surrendered to the lord of the manor as a way
of transferring them to another holder, or at the end of a
lease for a specified number of years. It is clear that at
least 21 of these were, in fact, sales of copyhold estates
for cash, and a number of others were surrenders at the end
of mortgage terms or leases. Twenty-four, or just under
half, were transfers by inheritance between kin. This was
not a simple 'peasant' society with families holding on to
ancestral plots for generation after generation. The results
can be seen in the rapid turnover of family holdings. Of the
274 pieces of property in the two Earls Colne manors in a
rental for 1677, only 23 were held by the same family
(female links included) two generations earlier in 1598.
This massive shift can be seen even in short periods.
Comparing two rentals for Earls Colne manor in 1549 and
1589, we find that of the 111 pieces of property listed at
the earlier date, only 31 pieces were in the same family
some forty years later. This is the case even if we trace
the inheritance of property through women. Property was very
mobile and there seems to have been no strong attempt to
'keep the name on the land' as in some other agrarian
societies.

We might expect a much less mobile situation in the
Cumbrian parish. Yet even in the north the turnover seems
to have been considerable. For the chapelry of Lupton the
earliest manorial records date from 1642 and the list of

tenants for that year gives 28 different surnames. Some two generations later, in 1710, only 12 of these surnames have survived among the property holders in the chapelry. Of course, changes of name at marriage would be likely to be missed by such calculations and hence family continuity is likely to be higher than this suggests. The only way to study the problem properly, and this is feasible, would be to study each holding over the period.

The penetration of the market into both areas is also shown by the web of debts which becomes visible through the use of probate inventories. After cataloguing possessions, these documents often have a list of both incoming and out-going debts. A brief analysis of such lists of debts illustrates for the northern parish that rather than being the isolated, rural, immobile population which we might have imagined, the inhabitants had widespread contacts and that borrowing and lending was enormously important to them. Some indication of the dimensions of such loans may be given by looking again at the Middleton family at Aikrigg Green. John Middleton had at his death in 1586 movable possessions whose total value was £69 8s.4d., but he was owed another £66 6s.8d. in cash out on loan. A century later Robert Middleton's inventory records that he had movable posses-sions worth £51 2s.8d., owed other people £57 4s.8d. and was owed £170 0.0. Very often money lent out and borrowed was greater than all the household possessions, including livestock and tools, clothing and furniture. Some of the inventories not only list the debts but also the places where creditors and debtors lived. To give one example: the inventory of Edward Burrow, a Lupton 'husbandman' in 1603, gives a list of debtors who lived in the following places; Clarethorpe, Mosside, Barbon, Carnforth, Warton,

Underbarrow, Killington, Yealand, Dalton, Nether Kellet,
Kirkby Lonsdale, Arnside. Many of these were twenty or more
miles from his home parish. Other Lupton inventories mention
debtors in the south of England, East Anglia and elsewhere.
The main theories to explain such indebtedness concern the
need to spread risk in such a society, the shortage of cash
which led people to accept bills and bonds, and the
importance of such exchanges in both providing credit and
cementing social relationships. Among the problems to be
explored are the presence or absence of specific 'money
lenders' in certain parishes, a feature which can only be
studied at the level above a particular chapelry.

Along with indebtedness, another feature of agrarian
societies which we may examine in the past is the basic unit
of production. It has been argued in relation to other
agricultural societies, such as prerevolutionary Russia or
contemporary India, that most of the production and consump-
tion in such societies occurred within the family or
household. This feature, together with others has been
termed the 'Domestic Mode of Production' and has been well
described by Sahlins (1974: chs. 2, 3). Where this is the
case there are many interesting consequences, including the
way in which the amount of labour produced by a person
fluctuates to fit with the fluctuations in the domestic
cycle within the household. At first sight the economies of
Kirkby Lonsdale and Earls Colne would both appear to fit
within the category of the 'domestic mode'. Labour groupings
seemed to be based on no wider unit than the household:
there is little evidence from the documents or secondary
descriptions of collective or collaborative labour outside
the household. Yet closer examination of production soon
suggests that both areas were, in fact, in various respects

different from the classic accounts of such a system. The
Account Book kept by the lord of the manors of Earls Colne
and Colne Priory shows that the manorial system organized
a good deal of the labour through a combination of services
owed and cash payments for rent. The northern parish also
was organized to a considerable extent on a manorial basis.
Furthermore, the institution of servanthood, which moved
labour in and out of the households, also made the situation
radically different from the archetypal East European cases.

The situation becomes even less like the stereotype if
we examine the mechanisms within Kirkby Lonsdale in a little
more detail. It is true that most of the labour on the small
farms was family labour, and this was supplemented by farm
servants, but the important corollary that most of the
labour of the children went into their parent's holding does
not hold true. The stereotype envisages a situation where
all the children remain within the communally-producing
group, at least until the father dies. In this situation the
labour pool contracts and expands very dramatically over the
life cycle of the parents. In Kirkby Lonsdale farms,
however, the labour pool seems to have been kept at roughly
the same size by exporting the surplus children when they
began to be productive and, if necessary, hiring in
servants. How this worked can be shown by linking the parish
register and the listing of inhabitants in 1695. If we do
this, it is possible to construct a hypothetical 'listing'
which shows who would have been living in the parish if
children had stayed at home to help with the family farm.
To summarize the results briefly, it appears that of the
children born to couples mentioned in the Lupton listing and
not recorded as buried there, between one-third and a half
seem to have disappeared from the parish to live and die

elsewhere. Where these children went and for what purpose
is still a mystery. But clearly this phenomenon already puts
the English economy, so far as Kirkby Lonsdale is
representative, in a different category to historical India
or Russia. The contrast would not be so great if it could
be shown that such children sent their earnings home to a
communal account, but, as yet, there is little evidence of
this.

Another topic of central importance is the distribution
of wealth, between individuals and over time. Two tentative
preliminary remarks can be made about the sample parishes.
The first is that the amount of capital and the *per capita*
income increased considerably in the period between the mid
sixteenth century and the early eighteenth century. This has
already been implied by the changes in clothing, furniture,
debts and total movable wealth discussed in the pages above.
It is a well established and well known trend, documented,
for example in the 'housing revolution' of the later sixteenth century in the south of England, and in the solid
stone houses in Kirkby Lonsdale, which mostly date from the
seventeenth century (Barley in Thirsk 1967: ch. 10; Hoskins
1953). The other strong impression is that the distribution
of wealth *within* parishes became increasingly uneven during
this period, a trend which probably started, in the south
of England at least, before the middle of the sixteenth
century. A comparison of the two parishes suggests that by
the late seventeenth century the distribution was far more
uneven in the Essex parish than the Cumbrian one. Even
though Hearth Taxes tend to conceal some of the differences,
we may give a preliminary indication of the relative
inequalities by comparing the two areas. In Lupton in 1669
the majority of the population still lived in one-hearth

houses; only 7 out of the 37 houses listed had two or more
hearths. The largest was the one case of a three-hearth
house. In Earls Colne in the 1671 Hearth Tax there were many
more substantial houses. The bulk of the population (86
houses) still lived in one-hearth houses, but there were 27
two-hearth houses, 13 three-hearth, 11 four-hearth, 8 five-
hearth, 8 six-hearth, 2 seven-hearth, and 2 with more than
10 hearths. The gap between the landless labourers and
weavers and the 'gentry' was already established in this
Essex parish in a way which was absent in Kirkby Lonsdale.

The difference of wealth caused differential problems
of poverty in the two areas. The absence of overseers of the
poor accounts for both Lupton and Earls Colne before the
eighteenth century makes a really detailed analysis of the
problem of poverty less profitable than it might be. But
wills, churchwardens accounts and other sources make it
possible to gain some impression of the situation. Another
complication is the fact that it seems to have been the case
that some of the Lupton old and poor migrated into the
neighbouring market town of Kirkby Lonsdale, so that the
rapidly lengthening poor lists of the second half of the
seventeenth century for that town partly reflect changes in
the outlying chapelries. Yet the general impression, at
present, is that although the average income of those in the
Essex parish might be far greater, it is likely that the
problem of the unemployable and destitute poor was also
greater than in the northern parish.

The information for the study of economic behaviour
over long periods of time is plentiful in local records.
Only a few of the more obvious questions have been posed
here and other more difficult questions concerned with
motivation and attitudes have not been examined. The real

value of any community study on the subject of past
economics is that while many of the questions have been
asked before, the answers had to be sought in straight
economic terms. The interweaving of local records allows us
to search for part of the solution to economic behaviour in
realms other than the purely economic. Intuitively we know
that economic transactions were in many ways embedded in the
demographic, social, religious and intellectual forces of
past societies. In order to explain them we need to be able
to move into these dimensions. We may therefore turn to
other features of the past.

5:3 Population studies.

The large potential for demographic analysis contained
in historical records is now widely recognized (Wrigley
1966; Hollingsworth 1969). Whereas land records and
inventories provided the core of the economic analysis, here
the focus is upon parish registers and listings. There are
three levels of intensity in such analysis. Firstly, there
is aggregative analysis, which provides totals or 'aggrega-
tions' of various events such as births or marriages. Such
totals make it possible to work out crude rates. Secondly,
there are methods based on linking births (or baptisms),
marriages and deaths (or burials), together. This enables
one to construct far more satisfactory age-specific rates.
Thirdly, there is the possibility of linking such age and
sex-specific rates to other local documents so that the
findings can be further broken down by occupation, wealth,
religious affiliation or other features which appear to be
interesting.

There are various direct and indirect methods of
estimating the total population of a parish; some of these

may be illustrated for Lupton though the samples are too
small to have any statistical significance. They are given
to show what could be done with a larger sample, rather than
as concrete results. Arguments based on the figures are
examples of what might be argued. The figures are too small
to make the conclusions safe. One method is to take the mean
average number of births or baptisms in a period and to
multiply it by a likely crude birth rate for such a population. In Lupton during the decade 1691-1700 the mean annual
average was 6.1 baptisms which, if we assume a crude birth
rate of 40 births per 1,000 population, would mean that
there was a total population of 152 in the chapelry. Another
estimate can be obtained from using taxation listings. The
1674 Hearth Tax referred to 56 separate dwellings. There has
been much dispute about the correct multiplier, in other
words the likely number of persons living in each house. In
England generally, between four and five seems to be
accepted. If we take the lower figure, this would give a
total population at that point of 224, but this is far above
the parish register figure for the later period. Fortunately
in Lupton there are two more direct estimates. In 1692, the
Reverend Thomas Machell travelled through the chapelry and
noted that there were 56 'families' in the lordship of
Lupton (Machell 1963: 26). If we assumed that a 'family'
would have the same number of members as a household, and
again took a multiplier of four, we should get the same
large figure as before. Three years after Machell a listing
was made and some 54 separate 'households' (assuming that
5 of the 12 bachelors lived as separate 'families') are
shown. Yet the average size of these was so small that the
total population only came to 137 persons. Various tests
suggest that a few people were missed, so that a total of

about 145 is more likely, which accords well with the parish register estimate. Clearly the multiplier of four is far too high for this chapelry, and this is confirmed by looking at neighbouring listings in the same way.

We may view the Lupton findings within the wider context of Kirkby Lonsdale and note the impression gained from looking at the parish register from 1539 onwards and comparing the totals with the total population shown in the 1695 listings. From this it appears that although there was a growth in the total population in the second half of the sixteenth century, and there seem to have been some years of high mortality, particularly 1598 and 1666, the general pattern was already substantially different from that described for parts of France, Germany or even Scotland at that time. Instead of a rapid build up of population cut back by a 'crisis' of war, epidemic or famine, which in turn led to a drop in the age at marriage and a rise in fertitlity leading to another crisis, the Cumbrian pattern was different. There were indeed minor crises, but already some form of 'homeostatis' had been achieved (Macfarlane 1976b: ch. 16; Wrigley 1969: ch. 2). If this is correct, we may wonder whether the absence of a 'crisis' pattern was the result of restricted fertility, high annual mortality, out-migration, or a combination of these three.

We may first look at the simplest measure, the crude birth rate (CBR), or number of livebirths in a year divided by the total mid period population multiplied by 1,000. Here again the numbers are too small to be statistically meaning-ful and are only given to illustrate methods of argument. For Lupton in the decade 1691-1700, if we take the listing as accurate, this gives us a CBR of 44.5. Since this is extremely high we need to check it against other parishes.

Killington to the north has an excellent listing and its own
chapelry register. The CBR for Killington in the same decade
was 41, which confirms the general apparently very high
level. The well known drawback of this crude rate is that
it does not allow for differences in the age and sex structure of the population. A glance at the local listings shows
that there seem to be very many married couples and few
children; this alone would lead us to expect a high rate.
In order to check the real fertility levels we need to look
at specific fertility histories of married women. In situations of uncontrolled fertility, with early marriage and
reasonable diet, women are likely to produce between six and
ten live-births before they reach the age of forty-five.
Since women tended to be baptized in one parish, married in
another, and have children in a third, it is a long business
working out fertility histories for women who are mentioned
as married in the Lupton listing. The impression, and it is
no stronger than that, from half a dozen cases where the
marriage is recorded and the woman dies after the age of
forty-five in the parish, is that the number of live-births
per woman is very low. In the best three documented cases,
only seven live-births are recorded in all. Although there
may have been under-registration of births which have
escaped checks against other documents, it is still fairly
certain that women in Lupton were not producing anywhere
near their theoretical maximum of children.

Among the major possible reasons for this very lowered
fertility, the strongest two are probably delayed marriage
and some form of contraception. If we look at the Lupton
listing of 1695, we can find an age at first marriage for
fourteen males in the list. These varied from the youngest
at twenty-four and the oldest at forty-eight. The mean

average age at marriage was thirty-five. By any standards, marriage for males at what amounts to middle age is extremely late, and is likely to affect women's marriage age. Taking the females mentioned in the same listing, their ages at first marriage were as follows: 28, 25, 33, 30 and 45, giving a mean age of thirty-two. Even allowing for the exceptionally old case, it would appear that women were marrying at around thirty, thus missing some twelve years of maximum fertility. With such a small number of cases the random variation would be great and therefore these are merely impressions. Assuming that the last conception would occur, on average, when they were about forty, and that births occurred, on average, every three years, it is not difficult to see why reconstituted families and wills so often give a picture of two, three or four surviving children, rather than the possible half dozen or more. In contrast, in Earls Colne taking a sample of people throughout the period whose surname began with the letters S to W, we find that the mean age at first marriage for eighteen men was 25.8, and for twenty women was 24.4. If this impression is supported by further research, the reasons for the difference would repay analysis.

In order to see whether as well as late marriage, contraception of some kind played a part, it would be necessary to work out age-specific fertility rates along the lines pioneered by Wrigley (1966). Since the calculations are so precise, a large base population is needed, the whole of Kirkby Lonsdale with over 2,000 inhabitants, rather than Lupton, for example. Taking such a large population should also make it possible to find out whether fertility rates differed between socio-economic groups; whether the occupational structure discussed above is reflected in differences of fertility, with certain groups marrying younger, having more children etc. In general, it seems clear that the much reduced fertility of the Cumbrian population goes a long way to 'explaining' the absence of a rapid population expansion, even though the late age at marriage (if this impression is confirmed) in itself needs to be explained. But mortality also needs to be examined in order to confirm the argument, since this might have checked population growth even more.

We may briefly look at two different aspects of mortality, particular crises and perennial mortality. A simple test for 'crises' years which has been suggested is that they are years when the mortality is more than double the mean average for the surrounding period (Schofield 1972). Applying this to Earls Colne, if we make a very rough calculation over the period 1560-1699 there were 2,605 burials in the 114 years when the burial register was complete, or an annual average of 22.85. Since the population expanded during the period, this would mean that in the sixteenth century any year with more than 40 recorded burials can be counted as a 'crisis', in the seventeenth, any year with more than 50 recorded burials. Using this criteria, only the years 1611, 1613 and 1635 were 'crisis' ones in Earls Colne between 1560 and 1699 though there may have been others in the 1590-1610 period for which the burial register does not survive.

It would be possible to look at particular years of high mortality and by using all the documents to find out the months in which the mortality occurred, which sex was most affected, the age of those who died, where in the village or outlying farms the deaths were, whether certain families were particularly badly stricken, and by these methods it is sometimes possible to work out the nature of

the diseases at work. The economic and social effects can
also be charted.

A second form of analysis is to examine mortality in
non-crisis years, either by examining all the deaths in a
particular period, or by looking at the life-histories of
a group of individuals (cohort) born at a particular time.
An example of the former would be to look at the crude death
rate (CDR), in other words the number of recorded deaths in
a year divided by the total mid period population,
multiplied by a thousand. If we do this for Lupton for the
1691-1700 decade, assuming the listing total of 137 to be
correct, we reach a figure of 39.5. Since this is again very
high even for a 'premodern' population we may look at nearby
Killington, where the rate was 33.8, again high but not as
extreme as Lupton. In Earls Colne, in contrast, even if we
assume a fairly low average population of 1,000 over the
whole period 1560-1700, the CDR would be the much lower one
of 22 (19 in the decade 1671-80). Since, as with fertility,
these rates are not only distorted by under-registration,
but also by the age and sex structure of the population, we
need to treat them warily. Furthermore, even if there was
apparently high mortality, we would want to know whether
this was mainly during infancy, adolescence, middle or old
age. A first impressionistic glance at the Lupton evidence
does not suggest a high level of infant and child mortality.
Taking all the children baptized as 'of Lupton' in the three
years 1694-7, in none of the 22 cases is a child recorded
as being buried within the first year, and only one within
the first three years. That this is not merely a result of
out-migration and loss of the deaths can be shown by the
fact that in at least eight of the cases we can follow the
children into middle age; two others died when they were

eight and nine respectively. Analysis of specific groups is also possible starting from an earlier point. For instance, if we look at the 26 males baptized as 'of Lupton' in the period 1660-9, we find that only three, or a rate of 110 per 1,000, which is fairly low by premodern standards, died within their first year. We can look at other recorded ages at death which are as follows: 18, 71, 28, 59, 38, 55, 67, 14, 61, 46. The outstanding feature about girl children is how difficult it is to trace them at burial. Of 25 girls baptized between 1660 and 1669, none were recorded as buried within the first year, but it is only possible to find a burial within Lupton for 3 of the 25, at 12, 18 and 62 years respectively. Again, the impression, to be confirmed or destroyed by further analysis, is of low mortality.

Another particularly vulnerable group would be women at childbirth and it is sometimes possible to pick out such deaths when a mother and child are buried on the same or nearby days. Again, a first impression from the Lupton evidence is that the rate was not as high as in many other societies. Of the four married women aged under forty-five in the Lupton listing whose age at marriage we know, and who continued in observation until they reached forty-five, having various children, none died in childbirth. The evidence of wills gives an impression that wives outlived their husbands more often than the other way round. It would clearly be possible, with a larger sample of women, to take this further.

We know that in many parts of England before the industrial revolution there was very considerable geographical mobility (Peyton 1915; Rich 1949; Schofield 1970). The presence of a parish register and listing for Kirkby Lonsdale makes it possible to add to this discussion, and to elaborate the findings discussed under the section above on the turnover of surnames of landholders. One suggestion of the mobility is that of the 20 males baptized in the period 1660-9 who had not been recorded as buried by the 1695 listing, only 6 were mentioned in the listing. The other 14 had gone to live elsewhere by the time of the listing. It is a further indication of the late age at marriage, that although all these men would have been aged between twenty-five and thirty-five at the time of the listing, not one of the six was married by then. All were listed as 'bachelors' though several subsequently married. Women, as we have seen, were even more mobile. Of the 23 girls baptized in Lupton in the same period 1660-9 whose death is not recorded in the chapelry, not a single one was there in the listing in 1695. A search for both boys and, especially girls, for the decades after this also suggest that very few stayed in Lupton after the first few years of their lives. A similar analysis of the Kirkby Lonsdale listing supports this impression (Macfarlane 1970b: Appdx B). In the absence of a listing, a much cruder analysis can be made on the basis of surnames in taxation records. Thus, of the 102 different surnames mentioned in Earls Colne in the Lay Subsidy of 1524, only 12 were present 150 years later in the 1673 Hearth Tax.

The movement away helps to explain the strange age structure of the Cumbrian chapelries. An age structure is the result of past fertility, mortality and migration, and it is therefore not surprising that the age and sex struc-ture of the two adjacent chapelries should be very different. It is impossible, at present, to accurately reconstruct the age of every individual in these northern listings because of the high geographical mobility. We may

therefore base our impressions on the categories of the
list-takers themselves. Looking firstly at the sex ratio,
in Lupton the name of children is not given, so we can only
work out the sex of adults. There were 56 males and 55
females; the imbalance was largely shown in the presence of
12 bachelors over the age of twenty-five. In Killington,
there was an exact balance of adults, with 80 of each sex.
Turning to the age structure, in Lupton there were 101
adults, either married or over twenty-five or both. Another
5 persons were said to be 'son' or 'daughter', rather than
'child' and it is possible to check the ages of most of
these cases and to discover that the distinction being made
was between young children, and those over the age of eighteen or thereabouts. In populations with high fertility, the
proportion sometimes reaches as high as a half of the
population under the age of sixteen which again indicates
controlled fertility and an elderly population. In
Killington there were 62 'children' to a total population
of 222, again an aged population. A curious feature which
differentiates the two chapelries is that while in Lupton
there were few widows, 3 of them as compared to 36 wives,
in Killington there were 15 widows to 42 wives. Whether this
was the result of earlier mortality of husbands, or pressure
against remarriage, would repay investigation.

5:4 Social structure.

The data for the study of social structure is more than
adequate. We may briefly survey a few instances to show some
of the questions one can ask. One of these concerns the size
and structure of the household, a topic which has attracted
considerable attention from social historians (Berkner 1972;
Laslett 1972). This work has shown that most Englishmen from

the middle of the sixteenth century onwards lived for most
of their lives in small households with a mean average size
of 4.5 and a simple structure consisting of parents and
children. The analysis of the Kirkby Lonsdale listing
confirms these findings. Although there is the problem of
where to place bachelors over twenty-five, who are often
listed separately, even on the assumption that each bachelor
shared a house with probably unrelated persons, the mean
household size for Lupton would have been under three
persons. The same is the case in Killington, which has a
more detailed listing, and where the 222 persons appear to
have been living in about 76 separate 'households', again
an average of under 3 per household. Not only was the
household very small, it was very simple. None of the
inhabitants of Lupton lived in households of more than two
generations depth; there were no cases of widowed mothers
living with their children, of uncles and aunts, or other
distant kin sharing a house, or of brothers living jointly.
The same absence of anything wider than the nuclear family
is shown in the neighbouring listings. It would thus seem
that it must have been the case that children did not marry
until their parents were dead or had retired elsewhere.

Such is the view of household structure from a listing,
but those who have used wills as their main source sometimes
argue that they, and manorial transfers, contain provision
for elderly parents and seem to imply multi-generational
households (Spufford 1974: 114). Kirkby Lonsdale provides
an excellent setting to see how the two findings can be
reconciled. If we look at the 115 surviving wills for Lupton
in the period 1550-1720, we find that in 29 of them, that
is between a quarter and a third, testators left wills
mentioning that they had married children; in nearly

three-quarters of the cases there were no children or they
were unmarried. The majority of these married children were
daughters; twenty mention married daughters, eleven mention
a married son. Daughters would normally have married out of
the parish, so we would not expect such marriages to cause
multi-generational households. Most of the sons may have
been younger sons and thus also living outside the parish.
Clearly there were situations envisaged in the wills where,
for example, a son is instructed how to treat his shortly
to be widowed mother who, it is assumed, would be living
with him. Unfortunately, the Lupton sample is too small to
generate many cases where this occurred just before the 1695
listing, but taking Kirkby Lonsdale as a whole should
produce some answers. What does seem to be the case is that
nowhere, either in the listings or the wills, is it
envisaged that two married couples would reside together in
one house. Sons and daughters might marry and live
elsewhere, but a 'stem' family of married parents and
married child (and his or her children) living together is
conspicuous by its absence.

It is obvious that a sharp distinction needs to be made
between family and household; people may live with their kin
and not act jointly, they may live in separate households
but act as a 'joint family'. In order to take the discussion
of family structure further, therefore, we need to look
beyond the physical units of particular households. In many
societies an individual is surrounded by close and more
distant kin through blood, and affines through marriage. By
itself, a list of inhabitants cannot tell us whether this
was the case in the past, since it merely needs a marriage
to change a woman's name and hence to conceal a relationship. What we need ultimately to establish are various

indices of kinship and interconnectedness, similar to those devised for European villages by Emmanuel Todd (1976). Until this is done, a few impressions will have to suffice. If we take a Lupton family which dominates the local records, the Burrows, we gain an impression of some kind of dominant localized kin groupings. The presence of 'clans' has been suggested for the highland areas of England (Cowper 1899; 199-201; Thirsk 1967: 9, 15). Such a development clearly did not happen, for example, in the Essex parish. But if one looks closer at the local families in Kirkby Lonsdale also, both the large ones and those which move in for a generation or two and then die away, the impression that emerges is that the extent of groupings was never wide, that any such 'grouping' was constantly shedding children, and that the normal experience in this area of England was for an individual to be surrounded by people to whom he could trace no kinship relationship. This must remain an impression until more of the genealogical links, to be gathered from all the sources, have been worked out.

Even if people did live near their relatives by blood or marriage, kinship, which is a social not a biological matter, may still be unimportant for them. In order to see what the effective groupings were we can use various indirect indices presented by local documents. One of these would be to see who acted as witnesses in the numerous documents such as marriage bonds, transfers in the manor courts, wills and inventories. A brief analysis of those who witnessed the documents made by the Houseman, Baynes and Burrow families in Lupton during the sixteenth and seventeenth centuries does not suggest any evidence for the thesis that kinship links were important. The witnesses turn out to be neighbours rather than kin, usually from the same

parish but not known to be connected by blood or marriage
in any way. This sample of the witnesses of 23 documents
will need to be extended and superimposed on the hidden
genealogical links before the impression is confirmed or
destroyed. It could be argued that since many of the documents were concerned with wills and inheritance this would
necessarily be the case, since family members were often too
directly concerned and hence debarred from acting as
witnesses by law. Such a criticism would not apply to
borrowing and lending patterns. The earlier discussion of
indebtedness can be pursued to show whether it was from
neighbours or kin that a person borrowed; the present
impression from looking at many lists of debts in northern
inventories is that in very few cases were people of the
same surname mentioned, and even more rarely does a document
specify a kinship link. The evidence is still negative.

Another index of the importance of kinship in the past
is the nature of bequests made in wills. Although such
bequests are not a direct reflection of sentiment, for
example the closest relatives may have received their gifts
or property before the will was made and may therefore not
be mentioned at all, they do provide a preliminary guide to
the distance and direction of family sentiment. An analysis
of the Lupton wills made in the period 1661-70 gives an
impression of a narrow range of kinship ties. Almost all kin
mentioned were either children or grandchildren; in the 11
wills of the period, no aunts, no cousins, and no in-laws
were mentioned. The furthest people went was, in two cases,
to mention a nephew or niece, in one an uncle, and in four
cases to mention a child's spouse. A search through all the
115 wills for the chapelry only led to the discovery of the
following kin outside the direct line; 11 wills mentioned

nephews or nieces, 6 mentioned 'cousins', 2 mentioned an
uncle or aunt. The most distant relative mentioned was a
'brother-in-law's son'. Even brothers and sisters are seldom
mentioned in wills. There is an enormous emphasis on the
spouse and on children and if these are living further kin
are rarely mentioned. A survey of the Earls Colne wills does
not suggest a different picture there. Again this is all
negative evidence. It does not prove that kin were
unimportant, but it does not give us grounds for believing
that they were.

Two further indexes, which could be analysed in order
to see what the structure of the kinship system was, may be
mentioned very briefly. One is the kinship terminology, or
that part of it reflected in terms of reference. Here again
the wills are a prime source. The analysis of a dozen Lupton
wills starting with the letters A and B gives no evidence
that the kinship terminology was any different from the
'Eskimo' form which is current in contemporary England (Fox
1967: 258). Relatives are called brother, sister, nephew,
brother's daughter or sister's son, cousin, grandson or
granddaughter in exactly the same way as they are now. Such
a system stresses the line and makes the calculation of more
distant relationships very difficult. Another indirect
approach is through the naming patterns of the children. A
stress on the male or female line could well be detected
through the practice of naming sons and daughters after
certain kin. Again a preliminary examination of the
genealogies which can be built up by combining records,
although it gives a hint that certain Christian names did
run in families and that eldest sons and daughters were
often named after parents and grandparents, shows a great
deal of flexibility. There seems to have been a preference,

but no firm rule, which encouraged, for example, the eldest
son to be named after his paternal grandfather, so that one
would get a run of names. The Middleton family of Aikrigg
Green whom we met earlier have a run of John - Arthur - John
- Arthur. The patterns in female names would repay further
analysis.

Closely connected to the questions discussed above is
the sociology of marriage. At the simplest level there is
the physical distance between marriage partners. A good deal
of analysis has been undertaken to show, for example, the
amount of intra-parish marriage. Such analysis can be
undertaken whenever the parish register gives both partners'
parish of origin, or there are marriage bonds which give the
same information. In Earls Colne during the Interregnum both
partners' parish was given. Of the 40 marriages, in 24 cases
both came from Earls Colne, in 11 cases the male came from
outside, in 5 the female. The proportions were roughly the
same in the 1696-1705 period, but then in the period 1730-9
there was a dramatic change, with only 21 marriages in which
both were from inside the parish, 26 with the male from
outside, one with the female from outside and 25 with both
partners from outside. Further analysis would be needed to
see why this occurred, and to measure the exact distance
away of the outsiders. In Lupton, such calculations would,
in the period 1660-90, give us a smaller proportion of cases
where both were from Lupton, some 22 of 60 marriages,
reflecting the much smaller size of the population. Such
analysis is not as meaningful as it at first appears. With
the high rate of geographical mobility, although a couple
may be stated to be of the same parish at the time of their
marriage, their birth places might be far apart. Marriage
distance derived solely from parish resisters or bonds

cannot be used as an index of parish endogamy. This may be
seen by looking more closely at marriage partners who were
said to be 'of Lupton' at the time of their marriage in the
decade 1691-1700. Of the 8 males so designated, only 2 are
recorded as baptized in the parish. Of the 14 females, only
4 had been baptized in the parish. Even high rates of intra-
parish marriage can be reconciled with the idea that people
did not marry kin or close neighbours.

By combining information from all sources it is
possible to find out whether people of particular social
ranks married into the same level or whether there were
other sub-groups of a religious or other nature within which
marriages tended to occur. Furthermore, as has been realized
by geneticists, the historical material is often good enough
to be able to study physical inbreeding (Kuchemann *et al.*
1967). It will also be possible to discover whether there
were 'preferential' or 'prescriptive' marriage rules which
laid down, as they do in some societies, which kin a person
should marry. It seems likely that the situation in England
was a 'complex' one, where rules can only be studied at the
level of statistical patterns, and consequently these rules
can only be discovered after very intensive studies of
particular areas (Fox 1967: ch. 8).

One of the areas where there is most evidence it that
of sexual behaviour. Parish registers can be used to find
out whether women were pregnant when they were married (Hair
1966, 1970), and this can be supplemented by looking at the
ecclesiastical and civil court records where offenders were
presented. Consequently, a good deal of work can be
undertaken on bastardy, bridal pregnancy, adultery, sexual
slander and a number of other topics. The age and status of
those accused can often be ascertained. In Earls Colne, an

analysis of sexual offences in the 1580s has shown that
about a dozen incidents a year can be discovered in the
local records; many of those involved can be placed on a
map, and their family and other links to each other can be
traced (Macfarlane 1977: 10-18). It is therefore not
surprising that the study of sexual behaviour in the past
is increasingly attracting the attention of social
historians (Laslett 1977). It should one day be possible to
see how such behaviour fluctuated over time and to analyse
the ways in which it was related to weather, prices, changes
in popular morality and other topics.

Sexual behaviour is often connected to questions of
honour, so that in order to understand it we need to analyse
questions of status and prestige in past communities. The
analysis of social hierarchies is notoriously difficult.
While it may not be impossible to estimate the relative
wealth of different individuals, it is almost impossible to
estimate the effects of such differences on the way people
perceived themselves and others. Indirect indices, such as
differences in literacy, mortality, clothing, housing, need
to be used to establish whether, for example, a relatively
homogenous social structure in the later sixteenth century
had been transformed by the mid eighteenth century into one
where there were very wide differences in life style between
rich and poor villagers. For instance, those involved in
sexual offences in the parish of Earls Colne in the period
1589-93 seem to have come from all ranks of parish society;
vicar, schoolmaster, churchwarden, and wealthy villagers
appeared alongside and were often involved in scandals with
servants and the poor. By the end of the seventeenth century
in the same parish this situation appears to be
inconceivable. The 'respectable' element of the village was

by then thinking and acting in opposed ways. Their leisure and their work, their upbringing and their education, all seem to cut them off from the lower sections of the village. This seems to indicate that a transformation from a society based on rank to one based on class was occurring during this period, as has been argued in other terms by Keith Wrightson (1974).

Another way of studying similar problems would be to look at the distribution of titles and terms of address, for example, the gaining of honorifics such as 'Mr' or 'Esquire'. Furthermore, the tracing of particular families through time would show cases of both upward and downward mobility, in terms of both title and occupation. One of the difficulties of such analysis is that by studying social mobility over a number of generations, we have to take into account the fact that the society is changing around the individuals. A further problem is the fact that families did not move as a block; elder and younger sons might be mobile in different directions and, within a couple of generations, grandchildren might be at totally different levels within the village.

5:5 Law, politics and administration.

There has been a growing interest in recent years in crime and social control in the past. Local records provide copious information concerning many areas in this field (Cockburn 1977). The analysis of patterns of crime and litigation is enriched by setting the cases within their local context. Furthermore, until we understand how various courts worked at the local level and the way in which disputes moved between them, national and regional statistics are misleading. As we have seen in earlier chapters, numerous courts had jurisdiction over the inhabitants of villages in the past. An indication of the gross quantity of legal business which could occur is given in a brief examination of the records for the Essex parish for just five years, between 1589 and 1593. In these years, the following separate cases appeared in each type of court: Assizes (3); Quarter Sessions (10); Star Chamber (1); Court of Requests (1); Archdeaconary Court (158); Court Leet (48). It is not always possible to disentangle the cases or even to know, in those where persons were merely excommunicated for not appearing at the court, what the case was about. Therefore the numbers given here are approximate, but they do indicate that more than 200 legal actions, varying from proving a will in the ecclesiastical court, to theft, have left their mark over a five-year period, on this village of roughly 1,000 inhabitants.

The process of each court, the fees and fines paid and the nature of the compurgators and witnesses and its effectiveness in punishing individuals and maintaining order, can be studied from these records. To take one small example. It has been suggested recently that the court leet was ineffective by the end of the sixteenth century, the evidence being that individuals kept committing the same offence (Parker 1976: 158). If we examine the activities of the court leet for the Earls Colne manor and set them against the occasional bailiff's accounts, it is clear that the fines were being extracted and there is no evidence that the institution as a whole was merely a hollow formality.

It is clear that by the late sixteenth century each parish was already enmeshed within a complex administrative machine. Each court and every institution needed local officials to help to operate it. Through the records it is

possible to study the activities of vicars, churchwardens
and 'questmen', of bailiffs, decenners, beckwatchers,
aletasters, and numerous other manorial officials, of
justices of the peace, constables and overseers of the poor.
The duties and difficulties of such local officials acting
as mediators between outside powers and their neighbours is
shown in almost every document. Since what actually reached
the courts and was written down depended very heavily on
such officials and their ideas of the offices they held,
study of them is not merely a separate and dry piece of
administrative history.

Although the constable and churchwardens were important
in maintaining law and morality, it is well known that most
behaviour is not controlled by an elaborate hierarchy of
courts, but by informal sanctions, such as the need for
reciprocity, by scorn, ridicule, gossip, fear of cursing,
as well as positive inducements to good behaviour and child
socialization. Local records enable us to probe a little way
into this world of *charivari* and shaming and to look at some
of the forms of informal control along the lines pioneered
by Natalie Davies (1975; ch. 4). For example, we find the
use of gossip, slander and scandalous rhymes. In Earls Colne
in 1587 John Brand was presented at the Quarter Sessions for
spreading the following rhyme about a case of suspected
adultery:

Woe be unto Kendall that ever he was born
he kepes his wife so lustily she makes him wear

the horn
but what is he the better or what is he the worse
she keeps him like a cuckold with money in his purse.

Another example would be the fear of being bewitched or
being thought of as a witch. Suspicions of witchcraft occur

in the local records of both the Cumbrian and Essex parishes
taken as samples here (Macfarlane 1970a: cases 1002, 1037,
1129). Such cases were merely the surface; it is clear that
many fears never came to be written down. Unneighbourly acts
were likely to be controlled not only by the fear of
creating a bad reputation, but also by the belief in
mystical sanctions, sent either by God or ill-minded
persons. For we have to remind ourselves of a fact which can
be concealed by local documents, that this was a world where
the borderline between natural and supernatural, between
angry thought and physical damage, was not as sharply drawn
as it is today.

If we return to the more observable past world of
crime, we find that village records enable us to construct
maps and graphs of particular crimes over long periods. But
it is only by combining the records of all the courts and
of other local documents that we can gain some idea of what
these patterns mean. We may examine this by looking at the
crime of 'theft' in Earls Colne during the ten years from
1589. Eleven cases of theft are recorded, seven in the
Assize records, three in the Quarter Sessions, one in the
court leet. This number is too small for anything except an
impressionistic account, again to show what could be done
rather than providing usable results. The occupations of the
accused can be checked against other records and seem
substantially accurate, and furthermore it is clear that
they did live in Earls Colne when stated to be of that
place. Most of the accused seem to have been at the lowest
level, tinkers, labourers, with one or two artisans such as
tailors and carpenters. The thefts seem to have occurred
mainly in the spring, and to have consisted of cloth, small
animals and furniture. The 'victims' appear to have been,

on the whole, wealthier. Throughout such analysis it must always be remembered that the records may be spurious and that we are at several removes from what actually occurred. To pursue the analysis further we would need not only to examine the victims in as much detail as the accused, and to see what relationship there was between them, for example whether there had been a previous history of dispute, but also to see whether the incidence of various types of offence altered over the seasons or over longer time periods. This would enable us to see, for instance, whether high food prices were correlated with food thefts.

Local records are far less helpful in the study of national politics than in the study of law. Civil wars and revolutions can occur, the Armada can be fought off, governments come and go and yet nothing appears in such records. It is sometimes inferred from this that villagers were uninterested and ignorant about anything other than local matters, that they were not part of the 'political nation'. It is only when, by chance, a record of a special kind survives that we realize that this is not the case. In Earls Colne, Josselin's diary covering the mid seventeenth century immediately shows that the vicar and many of the villagers, not only the rich and powerful ones, were constantly reading about and discussing politics (Macfarlane 1976a). Such interest stretched beyond the county level to national even to international affairs. It could well be argued from this and similar documents that the state of political awareness was higher, if such things can be measured, than was to be the case again until the advent of television in the mid twentieth century. The local records do not note national events because parish registers, wills and manorial transfers are not the place to do so. Likewise, in Kirkby

Lonsdale, the larger world would seem to have passed by the inhabitants, leaving scarcely a ripple, if we were not by chance reminded of it by the occasional Quaker prosecution or letter about political disputes. For these reasons it is impossible to make a systematic study of 'grand politics' at the local level. Only in the later eighteenth century and onwards is it possible to study even the very formal matter of voting patterns of the wealthy from poll books. A much more productive form of analysis from such records is the study of what might be termed 'micro-politics' or 'local-level politics'.

Such analysis is concerned with the distribution and use of power at the local level, whether that power be in origin religious, economic or social. The focus is on occasions when such power, usually concealed, becomes visible in a particular dispute such a a riot or civil litigation. The analysis is based on the 'case-study' approach, and deals both with the process of conflict and the factions involved (Van Velson 1967). The best material for such analysis lies in the often immensely detailed depositions and counter-depositions contained in the central courts concerning supposed offences. An example from Earls Colne would be the roughly 30,000 words in a set of depositions in a Star Chamber case that continued from 1606 to 1608. This describes a dispute over Colneford Mill when armed bands tussled in the village street. In Kirkby Lonsdale, the numerous Chancery cases provide similarly detailed material, as do the Assize depositions, part of one of which has been illustrated earlier in this work. Taken in isolation, such accounts have little meaning, but seen within the framework of other disputes and other records the dispute shows for a few days or months the nature of the forces which normally

lie concealed within the formal documents. The long drawn
out and bitter struggle between Quakers and their
prosecutors in Kirkby Lonsdale would be susceptible to such
analysis, which has already been applied with good effect
to witchcraft prosecutions in North America (Boyer and
Niessenbaum 1974).

5:6 Education and religion.

Commenting on the state of Cumbria, two eighteenth-
century authorities stated that 'it is a rare thing in this
county, to find any person who cannot both read and write
tolerably well' (Nicholson and Burn 1777: 9). We may wonder
whether this was indeed the case, either for the eighteenth
century or earlier, in the north of England. Here we will
be discussing another topic which has received a good deal
of attention recently, namely the ability to sign documents
(Schofield 1968). Among the sources for the study of signing
ability are the records produced for probate; wills, bonds
and inventories. If we look alphabetically at the first 60
male will-makers in Kirkby Lonsdale, we find that almost
exactly half signed their wills. This would appear to be a
far higher proportion than is the case for women. Of the 10
women whose signing ability is indicated in the wills they
made in Lupton between 1550-1720, nine made a mark, and one
put her initials on the document. This low figure is
paralleled in Earls Colne, where of the 16 women who made
wills and whose signing ability is indicated, between the
same dates, only one, a 'gentlewoman', signed her will, the
rest made marks. Earls Colne men in the period 1630-40
signed their wills in 5 cases and marked them in 7. One
objection to the use of wills is that the will-maker was
often old and might, especially in illness, make a mark

where earlier in his or her life a signature would have been made. We must therefore look at other documents. Administration bonds were made for women when they were left with an estate at their husband's death, and though they may not have been young, they were probably in good health. Looking at the Lupton bonds, of 45 women whose signing ability is indicated, there are 36 marks and 9 signatures. This does show a higher ability to sign. Another index would be the signing ability of the witnesses to wills. Looking at the witnesses to Lupton wills of persons whose surnames start with A and B, in 53 out of 57 cases where signing ability is indicated, the male witnesses did sign the document, thus indicating a far higher signing ability than that shown by the will-makers. Initials are rarely employed in any of these documents.

It has frequently been pointed out that those who made or witnessed wills were not representative of the population as a whole, since they were likely to be above average in wealth and status. It is therefore helpful if some other document can be used to reach the lower strata of the population. Fortunately there survives for Earls Colne a very full 'Association Roll', which is a list of signatures or marks of those who thereby showed allegiance to William and Mary in the year 1696. It is likely that the 160 names of males for Earls Colne represents more than two-thirds of the adult males then residing in the parish; this can be seen both from the likely total, given the age and sex structure of the population, and from the 35 or so other adult males shown by other records to have been living in the parish at the time, who are not recorded. Yet by reconstructing the background of those who did indicate their allegiance, it seems clear that there is a good cross-

section from the very poor to the wealthy. We find that 92
made a signature, one gave his initials, and the other 67
made a mark. It will be possible, by further investigation
of this document within the local context, to see how
signing ability varied with age, social status and other
factors.

It is one thing to be able to sign a document and
another to be able to write. Wills again provide at the
local level the best indication of writing ability, and recent work has shown that it is sometimes possible to find
out who were the particular scribes of wills, to compare the
handwriting of particular documents so that they can be
divided into those written by particular persons. This
methodology was developed by Margaret Spufford (1974: ch.
13). If we apply this technique to the Earls Colne wills,
for example, we find that at least half a dozen scribes can
be identified as writing more than one will. William Adams,
the son of a former vicar of Earls Colne, wrote seventeen
wills during the period 1625-62. Detecting such scribes is
not easy, for three reasons. Firstly, both in Kirkby
Lonsdale and Earls Colne, they do not seem automatically to
have acted as witnesses or put their names at the bottom.
It is therefore not possible simply to look at the
witnessing patterns as a guide to writers. Secondly,
handwriting seems to have varied considerably over a
scribe's lifetime. This is well illustrated in the case of
the vicar, Ralph Josselin. If his diary had not survived to
show the steady deterioration and alteration of his hand,
it would have been impossible to be confident that he wrote
the four wills for which we know he was the scribe. Finally,
and this is a point we will return to, the form,
particularly the introductory religious preamble, was not

standard and specific to particular writers.

It is generally agreed that the ability to read is
acquired earlier and more widely than the ability to write;
writing and signing therefore provide a minimum threshold
of reading ability. Unfortunately it is only indirectly,
through book publication figures or remarks by visitors,
that one is able to piece together an idea of reading
ability. Another indirect index is the presence of books in
the home, as shown in probate inventories of the period. A
study could be done for the approximately 2,000 Kirkby
Lonsdale inventories. Of the 146 Lupton inventories for the
period 1550-1720, 26 mention 'books'. The titles are only
specified once; 'Book of Martyrs, Eusebius and Josephus with
one great bible' valued at £3 10s. in 1679, owned by a
Quaker family. This is the largest valuation; the mean
average value through the period is less than 5s. per
instance. All but five of the mentions come from the post
1640 period. Recent authors have shown that ephemera,
particularly penny chapbooks and almanacs, were the most
popular reading, and it is therefore quite possible that
there was widespread reading, yet no mention of books in
inventories (Thomas 1971: 348).

It is also dangerous to use the incidence of formal
educational establishments as an index of either literacy
or education. It is probable that much of the instruction
in reading and writing went on outside schools. The records
of formal institutions survive for the historian and we are
therefore forced to concentrate on them. There is no
evidence of any school in Lupton in the seventeenth century,
yet the listing shows a 'schoolmaster' living in the
village. Both Kirkby Lonsdale and Earls Colne were well
known for their grammar schools and both schools are well

documented (Merson 1975). It is probable that only a tiny fraction of the boys and girls from the village would go to such schools so it seems formal schooling was not the only route to literacy. Detailed search of local records often turns up instances of private schools; for example, a man living with his scholars in a private house in Killington. The Quakers were especially anxious to give such private instruction. Since most children would pass through servanthood or apprenticeship, it may well be that it was during such training, rather than in a classroom, that they learnt to read and write. Though a full answer to these questions cannot be gained from local records alone, they do provide a corrective to an overemphasis on formal teaching institutions.

As we have seen in the reference to the Quakers, the ability to read and write both influenced and was in turn encouraged by certain religious movements. The Protestant stress on bible reading has been put forward as a reason for the desire to encourage literacy. The spread of new and sometimes heretical ideas was made swifter by the printing press and widespread reading ability. Yet before discussing changes at this level, we need to establish how important formal religion was.

It has been forcefully argued that sixteenth- and seventeenth-century villagers were disinterested in formal religion, did not usually attend church, and were enormously ignorant of the fundamentals of Christianity (Thomas 1971: ch. 6). Other historians working with local records have assumed that church attendance was more or less universal and that there was widespread religious interest and enthusiasm (Spufford 1974: 246-7, 319). It would appear to be easy to decide this issue, especially if we tie it down

to whether people actually attended church or not. Yet
further search of the records suggests that it was only
rarely and by chance that we find concrete evidence on the
subject. Fortunately, Earls Colne is one place where such
evidence survives. At first sight there appears to have been
conformity and attendance. The ecclesiastical officials were
instructed to present those who did not attend their church
on Sundays and Feast days. Consequently, numerous cases
appear in the archdeaconary court concerning Earls Colne
villagers who failed to appear. Over the period 1561-1640,
despite one or two short gaps in the court records, some 93
males and 31 females were presented, once or several times,
for not attending divine service or communion. There appear
to be two peaks in such presentments, one in the 1590s and
the other in the 1630s, both of them times when the
ecclesiastical authorities are known to have been making
attempts to improve discipline. Detailed analysis of those
who were presented would tell us whether they were from all
levels of the village, or whether the churchwardens picked
on the poorer or the wealthier. Statements made by the
villagers in mitigation, concerning their illness or work
commitments, also help to give us some idea of whether it
was considered normal to attend. Unfortunately, church
records in themselves are ambiguous since they do not merely
reflect rates of non-attendance, but also the zeal of the
authorities. To assume that all those who did not get
presented in the courts necessarily attended would be
foolhardy and this can be shown dramatically for the period
when the vicar, Ralph Josselin, kept his diary.

    The ecclesiastical courts were not held in the first
years of Josselin's ministry, but during the last twenty
years of his time in Earls Colne, they merely mention 13

people as being presented from the parish for non-attendance
at church. We might have assumed that this indicated a full
church for the zealous pastor, and the religious preambles
to wills and references to godly meetings which Josselin had
with some of his devout neighbours might have strengthened
this belief. Given a parish of roughly 1,000 persons, even
if only those over the age of fourteen attended church,
there should have been a congregation of at least 500
persons. Yet when Josselin gives figures, they are far below
this. He frequently laments the 'thinness' of the congregation, and in January 1663 he noted 'not an 100 people
hearing the word' and the following January 'about 80 or 90
hearing the sermon'. Over four-fifths of the adults had not
attended, though the fact that it was January in an unheated
church might have been a contributory factor. Holy Communion
became a restricted rite, for the 'saints' the special band
of ardent believers. Having ceased to offer the bread and
wine in church for some years, Josselin noted that in April
1669 20 people were present at the Easter Communion, a year
later there were only 14, and at Easter 1674, only 12
persons and himself, finally at Easter 1680 there were 4 men
and 13 women (Macfarlane 1976a). It is thus possible to
argue both that non-attendance and ignorance were
widespread, and also that among a small group, and among the
growing number of non-conformists, religious enthusiasm
burnt strongly.

One of the reasons for apathy was the splitting of the
Church, first away from Rome, and then into non-conformist
sects. The religious formulae of wills have been used as one
way to find out exactly how such a process occurred, for
example to show how Roman Catholic references to Mary and
the Saints lingered on into the seventeenth century in the

north (Dickens 1964: 191-2). Such a study of the survival
of Catholicism in the two sample areas is possible, and it
might be feasible to apply this technique to a later period
to see whether religious sub-groups, for instance the
Quakers or Presbyterians, could be identified from their
wills. Once we have assembled a list of local Quakers from
the books of sufferings, Quaker registers and other documents, it is possible to look at the formulae in their wills
to see whether they show any singularity. All such analysis
must take into account that the formula is not a direct
reflection of the testator's spiritual state, since, as has
been pointed out, the scribe may be more important in
deciding what was written down. Yet a glance at the formulae
written by one Earls Colne scribe, William Adams, mentioned
above, is moderately encouraging in that although there are
constant features, the expression, like the handwriting,
varies considerably. It would not seem that the introduction
is purely the result of the scribe's training, or of his
following a set manual.

The discussion so far has concentrated on the more
external aspects of religion. The most interesting realm is
the actual set of beliefs and perceptions of which Christian
preoccupations only form a part. A feature which strikes one
forcefully when working on ecclesiastical records is that
there was a constant battle between the sacred and the
prophane, both in relation to time and space. Certain times
were 'holy' and religious, particularly the Sabbath, and
these should not be prophaned by certain behaviour. This
topic has attracted considerable attention from national
historians (Hill 1964: ch. 5) for the seventeenth century,
but the local battle between Sabbath breakers, those who
married in forbidden seasons, or failed to keep the Lenten

food prohibitions would make a most interesting study. In
Earls Colne over fifty persons were presented during the
years 1580-1640 for breaking the Sabbath by engaging in a
number of activities from football to harvesting. Most of
them conceded the general necessity of the rule, but pleaded
special circumstances. For example, in 1636 Edward Harris
was presented for selling beer in the time of divine
service, and his wife came to court and explained that she
and her husband were at church, and that 'there came one for
a little beer for one that was sick, which was (taken) by
a little girl that she left at home'. Another index of
attitudes would be the observance of the prohibited marriage
seasons. It has already been shown that in seventeenth-
century France, whereas county people abstained from
marriages in Lent, in Paris this was not observed (Goubert
1960: ii, 66). In the northern parish of Lupton during the
years 1650-1720 some 89 marriages were recorded, including
8 Quaker marriages. Not a single one took place in March,
which was prohibited for marriages as part of Lent. In the
south, of 283 marriages in Earls Colne between 1642 and
1720, 18 of the marriages occurred in March. In this case
there was a total absence of March weddings in the period
1667-94, but they were spread out evenly over the rest of
the period. Further study would show who deviated from the
rules and might suggest changing patterns.

We might go beyond the forbidden seasons, to look at
whether folk traditions concerning lucky or unlucky days
also influenced behaviour (Thomas 1971: 735-45). If we look
at the days on which the vital events of baptism, marriage
and burial occurred in the two areas, we find the following.
In Lupton between 1661 and 1700, marriages occurred on every
day of the week, with the notable exception of Friday, on

which there was only one marriage, as opposed to 10 on
Sunday, and 11 on Thursday. There was no especial favourite.
In Earls Colne over the period 1691-1700, no marriages
occurred on Friday, while Thursday with 15 marriages (other
days averaging about 4) was very popular. Turning to
baptisms for the same periods, in Lupton Friday was again
unpopular with only 3 baptisms, whereas other weekdays
averaged 11. But by far the most popular day was Sunday with
149 baptisms. In Earls Colne there was a contrast in that
Friday was not avoided and though Sunday was popular with
82 baptisms compared with an average of 25 for weekdays, the
situation was not as extreme as in Lupton. Burials in Lupton
were the one event which seemed to be spread out randomly
over the week, with no concentration or absence on
particular days, suggesting that the interment was not
delayed. Again, Earls Colne was not exactly similar in that
though the burials were spread out evenly over the rest of
the week, Friday had a total of 15 burials which was less
than half the average for the rest of the week. Further
analysis of the people who chose lucky or unlucky days
should be possible, and the small numbers improved by taking
the whole of Kirkby Lonsdale rather than just Lupton.

There was also a division of space into holy and
prophane, though we find in the church records a notable
disregard in practice for the sanctity of holy ground. The
churchyard in Earls Colne was used for football, as a
fighting area, a place to graze pigs, and for many other
purposes. The church itself was the scene of scuffles, a
repository for weapons and firefighting equipment and in an
extreme case a William Allen was presented in 1637 'for
pissing in the clock chamber so that it ran down and annoyed
the church'. The aura of grave sanctity and holy dread which

tends to surround such buildings now may well be a fairly
recent phenomenon, the result of their growing disuse and
nineteenth-century romanticism.

One reason for treating the church and the churchyard
with care was that they were the repository of the dead, the
bridge between the living and the world of spirits. The
attitude towards death and the dead in the past is an
intriguing subject and one where information from local
records can only partially fill in the picture. One aspect
upon which local records throw light is the cost of funeral
rites. Such expenses, an indirect index of how much a
society values the dead, are sometimes recorded in
inventories and accounts. In the 144 Lupton inventories, 19
mention funeral costs. The sums vary from 20s. to £7, with
a modal average of about £3. When we compare this with the
total value of just the movable goods of the deceased, which
in these cases averaged over £72, it will be seen that,
especially in comparison with some societies where there is
a vast expenditure in funeral ritual, little was spent.
Given the cost of digging the grave, the coffin, the woollen
or linen shroud, it is likely that a very large number of
guests could normally have been entertained. Indeed the
documents are singularly silent concerning the wake and the
mourning relatives whom one would find in neighbouring
Celtic societies. Secondary sources have, so far, shown
little evidence of keening in England, or elaborate ritual.

Another curious feature in a comparative perspective
concerns the placing of the graves. Wills sometimes lay down
specific instructions as to where individuals were to be
buried. The usual formula was that it was to be in a certain
churchyard and occasionally near a deceased spouse or
parent. A walk round the graveyards of these parishes, as

well as published studies of graveyard inscriptions suggest
only a little patterning of the graves and then mainly for
gentry families. In death, as in life it seems, the kinship
pattern produced no discrete groupings.

Nor is there evidence of any especial interest in the
dead once they had departed. Although witches and witchcraft
were important as supernatural forces, the fear of ancestral
curses, or of ghosts, both of which are very important in
other religious systems, find little reflection in local
records, or at the national level. Instead, the graves seem
to have been under the charge of officials, the
churchwardens, and no money was usually left for their
upkeep in wills, except again amongst the gentry. Their
condition, as shown in ecclesiastical visitations, was
frequently very bad, the graves decayed, rooted up by
livestock, the stones upturned, the grass uncut. We need to
be aware of the distortions caused by local records and need
to set them against the occasional remarkable accounts of
beliefs concerning death and the dead which survive for
later periods (Atkinson 1891: 213-33). Yet even the intimate
diary of Ralph Josselin, though it gives a moving picture
of individual grief and mourning over children and near
friends, and of the pomp of gentry funerals, reveals no
interest whatsoever in the activities and fate of ancestors
or the dead. Once a person was buried, he or she seems to
have had little effect on the living.

5:7 Conclusion.

It has been impossible in this brief survey to cover
more than a small number of the topics upon which local
records throw light. Amongst those areas which could be
enlivened by local evidence are the following: concepts of

purity and impurity, of decency and indecency, of private
and public behaviour; attitudes to the poor, women, children
and other weak groups; leisure, games, ritual. The world of
prayer, spells, magic, astrology, fairies and demons which
we now know surrounded the physical world of the past is
also largely missing from this survey. Local records would
not answer any questions in these fields in much detail, but
a combination of such with other sources would help to probe
into the unspoken and hence unwritten assumptions of a
vanished society. Such records are also amenable to
linguistic analysis, and to examination by those who are
interested in subjects varying from what makes people laugh
to what symbols they manipulate. We have only just begun to
explore the value of the documents relating to particular
reconstructed communities, whether they be in sixteenth- and
seventeenth-century England, medieval Italy, or eighteenth-
century India.

Chapter 6

VIRTUES AND DEFECTS OF THE RECORDS AND THE METHOD

6:1 The records.

A good deal has been said in this book in praise of the
historical data for English communities in the past.
Although it would be difficult to prove, the experience of
one of the authors as a social anthropologist suggests that
the amount we can learn about people such as Henry Abbott,
a seventeenth-century villager, compares favourably with
what a social anthropologist can gather about members of a
community in which he resides. Naturally, the data is
different in many ways, but in sheer quality and quantity
it would be difficult to show that, except with particular
informants, the anthropologist can learn more. Furthermore,
it would seem likely that we can learn more about
individuals living some three hundred years ago than we can
find out from written records concerning contemporary
inhabitants of modern England. If we take into account the
difficulties caused by rules of secrecy and the high
geographical mobility of modern populations, it is difficult
to see how we could learn as much about people still living
as about those dead for several centuries, at least in the
absence of full-scale anthropological investigation. The
other major difference is the sheer size of the sample. It
is seldom possible for one social investigator to learn
about more than a few dozen, or perhaps, at the outside, a

few hundred, human individuals, in any real detail. Even
these individuals are only observed for one or two years of
their lives. The historical material enables us to trace
thousands of individuals, rather than tens, and to follow
them through their whole lives in a number of cases. Both
in terms of quality and quantity there is much for a modern
sociologist or social anthropologist to envy, though a
historian will also envy the sociologist's ability to ask
questions, to create his own data.

Yet with all its virtues, the particular material we
have been considering has a number of serious defects and
it would be unrealistic not to consider them. They can be
listed briefly, though each is a serious hindrance. One
problem is the archival and technical one of record loss.
Even the best documented parish will have large gaps in most
sets of records. Though one of the advantages of multi-
source work is that at least it makes it possible to gain
some idea of the dimensions of the loss, and to cast some
thin bridges across the chasm, the holes remain. For
example, for Earls Colne, the loss of the burial register
for the years 1590-1610 and the loss of the original court
rolls for some of the fifteenth and sixteenth centuries are
each a cruel blow. At the least, the social anthropologist
carries his most important data in his head, but the
fragility of the past is constantly made obvious by the
disappearance of documents we know once existed.

Another problem is the various ambiguities in the
records themselves. Often the ambiguity lies in the eye of
the beholder; as frequently stated, we do not as yet know
what many of the documents really mean and hence cannot use
them with confidence. This can often be resolved, we may not
know for a while whether appearance in a Hearth Tax means

that a person is living in a place or merely owns a house, but there are various tests which make it possible to find an answer. Much more difficult is the problem of the extent to which documents mean what they say. A notorious example is the whole area of 'legal fictions', whereby a completely fictitious account of an event that did not occur is devised in order to get round a legal difficulty, as in the case of common recoveries or riot. In fact, all legal records pose enormous problems. Since so much is at stake in many court proceedings, it is often almost impossible to be sure to what extent what is described as happening reflects any kind of objective reality. To use such records for statistical or other purposes is, therefore, extremely difficult. At least a social anthropologist has some faith in the evidence of his own eyes, but his caution with informants' statements needs to be shared, if not doubled, by the historian. These warnings concerning the untrustworthiness of documents are, of course, frequently made.

A separate problem is that some of the more complex documents, for example wills or manorial transfers, are themselves ambiguous. The English language, like any other, has a considerable capacity for ambiguity and it is often quite impossible to decide what a sentence means. For example, if punctuation is not used properly, it may be impossible to decide whether, in the statement 'John son of John the blacksmith', the occupation refers to the father or son. This problem of ambiguity, as well as the problem of meaning, is often partly masked from the investigator until he tries to break down documents in order to feed them into an indexing system, either manual or computerized.

Another defect in the data is that it comes in a set of discrete records and before it can be used for many purposes

these separate documents need to be linked or matched. An
investigator studying a contemporary community will probably
have little difficulty in deciding whether two pieces of
information relate to the same or different individuals, but
it is often much more difficult to do so when there are
thousands of small references to people in the past. Names
of one individual are often spelt in different ways; there
are frequently two or more people of the same name living
in a community; the information is sometimes vague; the
description of lands and houses often omits names
altogether. Considerable thought therefore has to be given
to the problems concerning record linkage. Even with much
care, it is not possible to identify unambiguously all the
individuals or other items mentioned in records, and hence
it is impossible to link them all together. Consequently,
there is always likely to be ambiguity in the final indexes.

The question of how to link records has received
considerable attention and there are now surveys of the
methods and literature (Wrigley 1973). In relation to the
methods described in this book all that can really confidently be said at the moment is that record linkage by hand
does seem to be possible, as the various experiments
described in chapters 4 and 5 have shown. Whether it will
be possible to achieve as good results using a computer must
await a later discussion.

A further defect in the data is that it is almost all
at the level of behaviour, describing events in the past,
rather than at the normative or cognitive level. We have a
very large amount of information about how people behaved
and interacted, but know far too little about what they
thought or said they were doing. This means that we can
generate very large amounts of statistical information, but

the reasons why people behaved in certain patterned ways can
only be guessed at. This is a curious reversal of the position of contemporary investigators, who often have a
plethora of data at the normative level - people's comments
on how one ought to behave, how people are thought to
behave, the reasons why people are thought to behave in
these ways - but rather little information about how they
actually do behave. Thus investigators are forced to infer
the statistical level from the normative data, whereas with
material of the kind we have been describing we have to
deduce the patterns of motivation from the patterns of action. Both types of inference need to be made explicit, for
they contain many concealed biases. Theories as to why
various patterns and rates occur in our sample population
will have to be imported from outside the data base.

It will be obvious that the material we have been
discussing represents only a tiny fraction of the past.
There are huge areas which are of interest to us and were
of importance to those who lived in previous centuries, that
are completely omitted in the records. Until we step back
from a community study for a moment, we may forget that
civil wars, scientific revolutions, the collapse of the
established Church, and even such locally important
phenomena as the weather or localized disease may leave no
obvious and direct trace in the records we have been
considering. The topics which never occur in such records
are far more numerous than those which do, and encompass
most of what is important to us and to our ancestors. Using
such records one gains only a very partial picture of some
very delimited areas of the past. This may be vividly
illustrated, for example, if we compare the account of
village life we would obtain from village records with the

account which, by chance, we have for seventeenth-century
Earls Colne in the shape of the diary kept by the resident
clergyman. This diary provides a picture of a world of religious turmoils, political activity, daily disease and illness, which is almost totally absent in the conventional
records (Macfarlane 1970b, 1976a).

Another weakness of the data arises from the fact that,
in reality, the geographical demarcation of a community is
artificial. On the one hand, we are aware that people were
highly mobile and consequently we often obtain only a partial description of any single life cycle. People move past
our bathescope window and then disappear into the gloom. A
second feature of this boundedness, connected to high
geographical movement in English communities as far back as
records exist, is the fact that economically, socially,
intellectually, and in every other way these parishes were
not isolated. Ideas, food, government, kinship sentiments,
all overflowed the parish boundaries. Although we may make
efforts to follow some of these chains outside the delimited
area, we are bound to oversimplify and impoverish the past
the moment we adopt the 'community study' approach. The
defects have been elaborated at some length in the introduction, where the reasons why both the nature of the data and
the need for a finite amount of information forces one into
adopting such an approach. There is therefore no need to go
over the ground again except to say that the intensive
analysis of the historical material, using the methods
sketched in above, does tend to give a spurious sense of
'community' boundaries which has to be consciously guarded
against.

A final bias which may be noted in the data is the
discrimination against certain groups in the population.

Particular categories, either because of their age, sex, occupation, wealth, or mobility, tend to be less well documented. The most conspicuous examples are women, and servants; but children, the poor and others are also less well recorded. Anthropologists often find that certain sections of the population with whom they live force themselves on their attention; they are easier to approach and easier to study. The same is true with the historical data. Although it is hoped that we will no longer suffer under the illusion that large sectors of the population in the past will always remain totally invisible, it is true that in relation to English historical communities, at least, even in the best recorded periods, it is the wealthy and males who crowd onto the stage.

All these defects in the data do not, we believe, invalidate the general approach. They do suggest that the community study approach described here is severely limited. It is one tool, among others, and not an end in itself. At present it offers hope of probing into areas which previous generations have thought were closed for ever. It provides large quantities of data of an unrivalled kind for literate societies stretching over long periods of time. With this material, sociologists, demographers, economists, biologists and others may test out some of their hypotheses. Yet, in the end, it will not, by itself, solve any problems except in combination with the numerous other sets of data and disciplines which are relevant to the study of man.

6:2 *General comments on manual analysis.*

It would seem that many interesting areas for investigation are closed to us if we do not undertake an extensive restructuring of the raw historical data. To this

extent, the method outlined above can be seen as an advance
on current techniques of community analysis. But there are
constraints of both a practical and theoretical kind in such
a hand analysis. These suggest that a complementary analysis
using computers would be worthwhile.

The first constraint is the practical one of the time
it takes to construct such a hand-indexing system. Earlier
we quoted an estimate that for a parish of 1,000 persons
over a period of 300 years it would take approximately 1,500
man-hours to undertake a full 'family reconstitution', based
on parish registers alone. The description of the nature and
quality of the data available has suggested that in terms
of names, perhaps one-tenth of those found in all the local
records come from parish registers. Furthermore, the entries
are simple and are easily transcribed and indexed. Taking
everything into account we might guess that the information
they include constitutes less than a twentieth of all that
contained. If this is correct, it would seem likely that in
order to bring a 'total reconstitution' up to the same level
as that desirable for a family reconstitution, in other
words to have all possible individuals, pieces of property,
families and other features linked together and ready for
subsequent analysis, would take anything up to twenty times
as long. If a single researcher worked for 30 hours a week,
50 weeks a year, it would still take 20 years to carry out
such a task, even for a moderately small parish. Even a team
of 5 persons would have to work for 4 years. Such lengthy
research and analysis, which has to be done before the real
historical work of substantive investigation can begin, is
clearly out of the question in terms of the way research in
social history is currently organized. It would also make
it quite impossible to undertake research on a region rather

than a parish, though the region is often a better unit for many social and economic questions.

In general, it would seem that the creation of the original indexes of unlinked persons and pieces of land would take about half as long by machine as it would by hand. If we make a rough estimate that it would take about 6 man-years to create the indexes for a parish of 1,000 persons for a period of 400 years, then it would take perhaps 3 years to process by computer. As yet, there would be no great saving. In terms of sheer processing of the data, rather than searching, the saving would come when further indexes were needed. For example, if an index by occupation were required, there would be practically no extra time needed if the data were in the machine already, whereas it might take months to create such an index by hand. A number of such more refined indexes will be needed in order to make the material really accessible even by hand. One of these indexes, which is crucial for many types of work, is an index by individuals, rather than by sets of persons who have the same forname and surname. This can only be produced on the basis of record linkage or individual reconstitution. It is this stage of deciding whether two pieces of information refer to the same or different persons which takes at least one-third of the total time in the preparation of data. To do this by hand for a file the size of the one which we have been discussing would probably add another 3 or 4 years onto the task. If it were possible to use the computer to link the records, even if it could only do this for 80% or 90% of the easier cases, would thus save perhaps 3 years work per community study. Taking all this into account, we might guess that such a project would require between 10 and 20 man-years from start to finish by

hand, or about 3 to 5 years (assuming that the computer
program were available) by machine. All these stages, of
course, are only preparatory. They only order the material
so that interesting questions can be asked. Searching the
data for answers to specific questions is the second area
where we can estimate the limitations of a manual-indexing
system.

The creation of hand indexes along the lines suggested
above makes the searching of data in order to answer questions much faster. It is possible to follow logical chains
fairly swiftly. Yet in terms of modern methods of data
retrieval, searching is still painfully slow. The historian
searches his files in two ways, sequentially and randomly.
In the former case, for example, he may want to search
through a parish register in order to lift out bastard
births, or through a set of inventories in order to see if
there is any correlation between the occupation of an
inventory-maker and the presence of certain implements in
the inventory. Using the files we have created, it would
take approximately four hours to search sequentially through
the typed parish register for Earls Colne from 1558-1837 in
order to look for registered bastards or other information,
even if one were reading very rapidly. The IBM 370/165
computer at Cambridge would take approximately six seconds
to search the approximately half million characters (letters
or numbers or spaces) involved. To search through and copy
out the appearances of a certain tool in the roughly 2,000
inventories for the parish of Kirkby Lonsdale would take
about twelve hours, assuming that the tool was mentioned on
average once in every 10 inventories and that the
inventories had already been typed to make them more
legible. To search the same file and copy out the same

entries would take the computer about thirty seconds in
'real time'. The central processing time is, of course, only
a tiny fraction of the total time the job would take on the
machine. Realistic estimates would have to include the time
taken to write the program to do the search, fetch the
results from the lineprinter and so on. Such considerations
mean that it is not usually worth undertaking a sequential
search with the computer if it would take under an hour to
do by hand. The economies of scale, however, are enormous.
For example, to search through the whole name index for some
missing cards by hand might take about thirty hours or more.
To write the program and locate such cards on the machine,
(though they would not, of course, have been lost in the
first place), would take well under an hour. The actual time
taken by the computer to search the whole file of over
100,000 entries would be under twelve seconds.

One variant of this sequential search frequently
employed by historians is the case where two or three
variables need to be plotted over time in order to see if
there is any correlation between them, perhaps in the form
of a moving graph. For example, one might want to test the
hypothesis that birth and death and marriage rates are
somehow interconnected over long stretches of time. The best
way to test this might be to produce a graph based on
aggregated figures from the parish register. To produce such
a graph, lifting out each fact one by one by hand, then
adding the numbers into totals, then drawing a graph, might
take one or two weeks to do for a parish of 1,000 for a
period of 300 years. To write the program and execute it,
once the data was in the machine, would not take more than
a morning using a computer. If one had added up the figures
by months in the original hand calculation and it was then

discovered that the figures were needed week by week, it is
quite likely that the whole process would need to be
repeated. Another week or two would be needed and the effect
on the researcher's enthusiasm would be considerable. If the
search had been done by the computer, a very slight
modification of the original program, perhaps taking an
hour, would make it possible to run the program again to
obtain the new results. This discussion of sequential
searching merely illustrates the very obvious fact that in
terms of sheer speed, a fast reader can read about 2,000
characters a minute. In the same period of time, a large
computer can read 5,000,000 characters. In other words, it
is over a thousand times faster than the human. Since the
historian is likely to want to extract considerable amounts
of information from various records in order to ponder over
them, the fact that the computer can type at over 1,000
(long) lines per minute, or about two hundred times faster
than a very good human typist, is also of relevance.

The most interesting searches through files are not
sequential but 'random'. In such cases, the investigator is
following a logical chain which cuts across the way in which
even the best of indexes is organized. For example, if one
is interested in following kinship links, or in discovering
who lived in a certain street at a certain time, or how old
various people were who happened to die in a particular
epidemic, it is necessary to jump around between different
kinds of files. Even to answer fairly simple questions, it
is often necessary to leap into various different sets of
files in order to find the relevant 'fact'. Some examples
of how long it takes to perform such random searching by
hand may be given. To build up the family tree and the pen
portraits of the Abbott family used in chapter 4 took about

50 man-hours of work, including many random searches. It is unlikely that the computer could ever do anything approaching the complexity of this task from beginning to end. Yet it could probably have printed out all the records in which the Abbotts are mentioned, and many background features of the family, in a few seconds. The difference is again a reflection of the relative speed of manual and computer searching. To find something by hand in even the best organized of filing systems takes a surprisingly long time. As an experiment, some 60 'random' searches were made by hand, looking for various different kinds of information The average time per search was about sixty seconds. The average time per random search using the indexed sequential system developed for our project at Cambridge is .2 of a second. This means that, in practice, a researcher has to think very hard indeed before he decides to undertake an analysis of any problem which will involve more than about 1,000 random searches. With a search time of one minute per fact, it will take a couple of days merely to find the data, let alone copy it out or think about it, when over 1,000 random facts are needed. For example, to conduct a search which involved correlating dates of death with acquisition of landholding by sons, if there were 1,000 cases and each involved 10 random searches, would take 166 man-hours by hand, even if we allowed only one minute to both find and copy each piece of information. To write the program, run it and obtain the results, should not take more than a day using the computer.

Since there are almost always hitches in running a program and there is the time spent in writing it, it is clear that it is often best to undertake small pilot studies by hand. For this reason alone it is absolutely essential

to have a complementary manual system, even if this is
partly or wholly produced by the computer. It is necessary
because many searches are too complex for anything but the
human brain to perform, with its enormous wealth of
knowledge about the way other humans behave, the historical
context of the documents, and many other sets of implicit
information. Yet it would also seem sensible to be able to
use both the sorting and searching power of the computer as
a tool in historical analysis. Certain tasks are best done
by hand, others are quite impracticable without a computer.
Yet it is one thing to dream about what a computer might do.
It is quite another to be able to convert the records we
have illustrated and analysed in this book into a form where
they can be sorted and searched by the machine, without
losing their complexity. A method of doing this will be
described in a sequel to this work.

BIBLIOGRAPHY OF WORKS REFERRED TO IN THE TEXT

Place of publication is London, unless otherwise indicated

Appleby, A. B. 'Disease or Famine? Mortality in Cumberland
  and Westmorland 1580-1640', *Economic History Review*,
  2nd series, xxvi (1973).

Atkinson, J. C. *Forty Years in a Moorland Parish* (1891).

Barley, M. W. *The English Farmhouse and Cottage* (1967).

Bell, C. and Newby, H. *Community Studies* (1971).

Berkner, L. K. 'The Stem Family and the Developmental Cycle
  of the Peasant Household', *American History Review*, 77
  (1972).

Bloch, M. *The Historian's Craft* (Manchester, 1954).

Boissevain, J. *Friends of Friends* (Oxford, 1974).

Bouchard, G. *Le Village Immobile* (Paris, 1972).

Barnes, J. A. 'Class and Committees in a Norwegian Parish',
  Human Relations, vii, no. 1 (1954).

Boyer, P. and Niessenbaum, S. *Salem Possessed: The Social
  Origins of Witchcraft* (Cambridge, Mass., 1974).

Campbell, J. *Honour, Family and Patronage* (Oxford, 1964).

Camp, A. J. *Wills and their Whereabouts* (1963).

Chagnon, N. A. *Studying the Yanomamo* (New York, 1974)

Cockburn, J. S. *A History of English Assizes 1558-1714*
  (Cambridge, 1972).

Cockburn, J. S. (ed.) *Crime in England 1500-1800* (1977).

Cowper, H. S. *Hawkshead* (1899).

Davis, John. *Land and Family in Pisticci* (1973).

Davis, Natalie Z. *Society and Culture in Early Modern France* (1975), ch. 4.

Dickens, A. G. *The English Reformation* (1964).

Dube, S. C. *Indian Village* (1954; reprinted New York, 1967).

Elton, G. R. *The Sources of History: England 1200-1640* (1969).

Emmison, F. G. *Elizabethan Life: Disorder* (1970).

Emmison, F. G. *Elizabethan Life: Morals and the Church Courts* (Colchester, 1973).

Emmison, F. G. *Elizabethan Life: Home, Work and Land* (Saffron Walden, 1976).

Evans-Pritchard, E. E. *The Nuer* (Oxford, 1940).

Firth, R. *Primitive Polynesian Economy* (1939).

Fleury, M. and Henry, L. *Des Registres paroissiaux a l'histoire de la population* (Paris, 1956).

Foster, G. M. 'Interpersonal Relations in Peasant Society', *Human Organization*, 19, no. 4 (Winter 1960-1).

Fox, Robin. *Kinship and marriage* (1967).

Frankenberg, R. *Communities in Britain* (1966).

Geertz, C. 'Form and Variation in Balinese Village Structure', *American Anthropologist*, 61 (1959).

Glasco, L. 'Comment on the Princeton Conference on Record Linkage', *Historical Methods Newsletter*, iv, no. 3, (June 1971).

Goubert, P. *Beauvais et le Beauvaisis de 1600 a 1730* (Paris, 1960).

Goubert, P. 'Local History in France' in Gilbert, F. and Granbard, S. (eds.) *Historical Studies Today* (New York, 1972).

Greven, P. J. *Four Generations: Population, Land and Family in Colonial Andover* (Ithaca, 1970).

Guide to the Contents of the Public Record Office (1963), 2 vols.

Guide to the Essex Record Office by F. G. Emmison (Chelmsford, 1969).

Hall, J. W. 'Materials for the Study of Local History in Japan' (1958), reprinted in Hall, J. W. and Jansen, M. B. (eds.), *Studies in the Institutional History of Early Modern Japan* (Princeton, 1963).

Hanley, S. B. 'Fertility, Mortality and Life Expectancy in Pre-Modern Japan', *Population Studies*, 28, no. 1 (March 1974).

Hair, P. E. H. 'Bridal Pregnancy in Rural England in Earlier Centuries', *Population Studies*, 20 (1966). Further examined in the same, 24, no. 1 (March 1970).

Hearnshaw, F. J. C. *Leet Jurisdiction in England* (Southampton, 1908).

Hey, David. *An English Rural Community: Myddle under the Tudors and Stuarts* (Leicester, 1974).

Hill, Christopher. *Society and Puritanism in Pre-Revolutionary England* (1964), ch. 5.

Hollingsworth, T. H. *Historical Demography* (1969).

Horsfall Turner, J. *The History of Brighouse, Raistrick and Hipperholme* (Bingley, 1893).

Hoskins, W. G. *Essays in Leicestershire History* (Liverpool, 1950).

Hoskins, W. G. *The Midland Peasant: The Economic and Social History of a Leicestershire Village* (1957).

Hoskins, W. G. *Local History in England* (1959).

Hoskins, W. G. *Fieldwork in Local History* (1970).

Jahoda, G. *Information Storage and Retrieval Systems for Individual Researchers* (New York, 1970).

James, Mervyn E. *Family, Lineage and Civil Society* (Oxford, 1974).

Kessinger, T. G. 'Historical Materials on Rural India', *Indian Economic and Social History Review*, vii, no. 4 (Dec. 1970).

Kessinger, T. G. *Vilyatpur 1848-1968: Social and Economic Change in a North Indian Village* (Berkeley, 1974).

Kessinger, T. G. 'Historical Demography of India: Results and Possibilities', *Peasant Studies*, v, no. 3 (July 1976).

Knodel, J. 'Two and a Half Centuries of Demographic History in a Bavarian Village', *Population Studies*, xxiv, no. 3 (Nov. 1970).

Kuchemann, C. F., Boyce, A. J. and Harrison, G. A. 'A Demographic and Genetic Study of a Group of Oxfordshire Villages', *Human Biology*, 39 (1967).

Laslett, P. (ed.) *Household and Family in Past Times* (Cambridge, 1972).

Laslett, P. (ed.) *Family Life and Illicit Love in Earlier Centuries: Essays in Historical Sociology* (Cambridge, 1977).

Leach, E. R. *Political Systems of Highland Burma* (1954).

Leach, E. R. *Pul Eliya, A Village in Ceylon* (Cambridge, 1964).

Legare, J., Lavoie, J. and Charbonneau, H. 'The Early Canadian Population: Problems in Automatic Record Linkage', *Canadian History Review*, liii, no. 4 (Dec. 1972).

Lison-Tolosano, C. *Belmonte de los Caballeros: A Sociological Study of a Spanish Town* (Oxford, 1966).

Lorwin, V. R. and Price, J. M. (eds.) *The Dimensions of the Past* (Yale, 1972).

Lucas, John. *History of Warton Parish, compiled 1710-1740*
    edited by Ford, J. R. and Fuller-Maitland, J. A.
    (Kendal, 1931).

Macfarlane, A. D. J. *Witchcraft in Tudor and Stuart England*
    (1970a).

Macfarlane, A. D. J. *The Family Life of Ralph Josselin*
    (1970b).

Macfarlane, A. D. J. (ed.) *The Diary of Ralph Josselin*
    1616-1683 (Oxford, 1976a).

Macfarlane, A. D. J. *Resources and Population: A Study of*
    the Gurungs of Central Nepal (Cambridge, 1976b).

Macfarlane, A. D. J. 'Historical Anthropology' in *Cambridge*
    Anthropology, 3, no. 3 (1977).

Machell, T. *Antiquary on Horseback: The Collections of the*
    Rev. Thos Machell, ed. Ewbank, J. M. (Kendal, 1963).

Maitland, F. W. (ed.) *Select Pleas in Manorial and Other*
    Seignorial Courts, i (Selden Society, 1889, ii).

Marchant, R. A. *The Church Under the Law: Justice,*
    Administration and Discipline in the Diocese of York
    1560-1640 (Cambridge, 1969).

Mayer, A. 'The Significance of Quasi-Groups' in Banton, M.
    (ed.) *The Social Anthropology of Complex Societies*
    (1966).

Merson, A. D. *Earls Colne Grammar School, Essex* (Colchester,
    1975).

Millican, P. *A History of Horstead and Stanninghall*
    (Norwich, 1937).

Mitchell, J. C. 'The Concept and Use of Social Networks' in
    Mitchell, J. C. (ed.) *Social Networks in Urban Situa-*
    tions (Manchester, 1969).

Nicholson, Joseph and Burn, R. *The History and Antiquities*
    of the Counties of Westmorland and Cumberland, i.

(1777).

Obeyesekere, G. *Land Tenure in Village Ceylon* (Cambridge, 1967).

Owen, D. M. *The Records of the Established Church in England, excluding Parish Records* (British Record Association, no. 1, 1970).

Parker, Rowland. *The Common Stream* (St Albans, 1976).

Pearson, Alexander. *Annals of Kirkby Lonsdale and Lunesdale* (Kendal, 1930).

Peyton, S. A. 'The Village Population in the Tudor Lay Subsidy Rolls', *English History Review*, xxx (1915).

Pitt-Rivers, J. A. *The People of the Sierra* (1954; 2nd edn., Chicago, 1971).

Postan, M. M. *Essays on Medieval Agriculture and General Problems of the Medieval Economy* (Cambridge, 1973).

Redfield, R. R. *The Little Community and Peasant Society and Culture* (1957; Chicago, 1965 reprint).

Rich, E. E. 'The Population of Elizabethan England', *Economic History Review*, 2nd series, ii (1949).

Ruston, A. G. and Witney, D. *Hooton Pagnell: The Agricultural Evolution of a Yorkshire Village* (1934).

Sahlins, M. *Stone Age Economics* (1974).

Schofield, R. 'The Measurement of Literacy in Pre-Industrial England' in Goody, J. (ed.) *Literacy in Traditional Societies* (Cambridge, 1968).

Schofield, R. 'Age-Specific Mobility in an Eighteenth Century English Parish', *Annales de Demographie Historique* (1970).

Schofield, R. 'Crisis Mortality', *Local Population Studies*, 9 (Autumn 1972).

Schofield, R. 'A Swedish Demographic Data Base', *Historical Methods Newsletter*, 7, no. 2 (March, 1974).

Shipps, Kenneth. (ed.) *Diary of Samuel Rogers*, edition in progress, Princeton.

Skinner, G. W. 'Marketing and Social Structure in China', part one, *Journal of Asian Studies*, 24, Nov. 1964-Feb., May 1965.

Spufford, M. *A Cambridgeshire Community: Chippenham from Settlement to Enclosure* (Leicester, Department of English Local History, 1965).

Spufford, M. *Contrasting Communities: English Villagers in the Sixteenth and Seventeenth Centuries* (Cambridge, 1974).

Srinivas, M. N. (ed.) *India's Villages* (New York, 1960).

Stacey, M. 'The Myth of Community Studies', *British Journal Sociology*, 20 (1969).

Steer, F. W. *Farm and Cottage Inventories of Mid-Essex 1635-1749* (Colchester, 1950).

Stephens, W. B. *Sources for English Local History* (Manchester, 1973).

Stone, Lawrence. 'Literacy and Education in England 1640-1900', *Past and Present*, 42 (Feb. 1969).

Styles, P. 'A Census of a Warwickshire Village in 1698', *University of Birmingham Historical Journal*, iii (1951-2).

Tawney, R. H. *The Agrarian Problem in the Sixteenth Century* (1912; Harper Torchbook edn., 1967).

Thirsk, Joan (ed.) *The Agrarian History of England and Wales 1500-1640* (Cambridge, 1967).

Thomas, Keith. *Religion and the Decline of Magic* (1971).

Todd, Emmanuel. 'Seven peasant communities in pre-industrial Europe' (Cambridge University Ph.D. thesis, 1976).

Tonnies, F. *Community and Association* (1887; translated 1955 by C. P. Loomis).

Turner, Victor. *Schism and Continuity in an African Society* (Manchester, 1957).

Van Velsen, J. 'The Extended-Case Method and Situational Analysis' in Epstein, A. L. (ed.), *The Craft of Social Anthropology* (1967).

Williams, W. M. *A West Country Village, Ashworthy* (1963).

Wolf, Eric. 'Aspects of Group Relations in a Complex Society', *American Anthropologist*, 58 (Dec. 1956).

Wrightson, K. 'The Puritan Reformation of Manners with Special Reference to the Counties of Lancashire and Essex, 1640-1660' (University of Cambridge, Ph.D. thesis, 1974).

Wrigley, E. A. 'Family Limitation in Pre-Industrial England', *Economic History Review*, 2nd series, xix (1966).

Wrigley, E. A. (ed.) *An Introduction to English Historical Demography* (1966).

Wrigley, E. A. *Population and History* (1969).

Wrigley, E. A. (ed.) *Identifying People in the Past* (1973).